The Autonomous System

The Autonomous System

A Foundational Synthesis of the Sciences of the Mind

Szabolcs Michael de Gyurky

with **Mark A. Tarbell**

Library of Congress Cataloging-in-Publication Data:

de Gyurky, Szabolcs Michael.
  The autonomous system : a foundational synthesis of the sciences of the mind / Szabolcs Michael de Gyurky, Mark A. Tarbell.
    pages cm
  ISBN 978-1-118-29424-6 (hardback)
1. Artificial intelligence. 2. Thought and thinking. I. de Gyurky, Szabolcs Michael. II. Title.
  Q335.T37 2013
  006.3–dc23

                                                        2013012064

Printed in the United States of America.

10 9 8 7 6 5 4 3 2 1

To the Voyager Project at the Jet
Propulsion Laboratory in Pasadena, California.

To its unforgettable crew members—the engineers,
scientists, and administrative personnel who facilitated
the encounters with the great planets of our solar
system—and our great captain, Dr. Edward C. Stone.

Above all, to the two Voyager spacecraft now
entering interstellar space, on their way into infinity.
Be well and safe, and remember us when we are long gone.

Contents

Preface

It can scarcely be denied that the supreme goal of all theory is to make the irreducible basic elements as simple and as few as possible without having to surrender the adequate representation of a single datum of experience.

—Albert Einstein[1]

WHY DESIGN AND BUILD AN AUTONOMOUS SYSTEM?

The subject of this book has long been designated the "holy grail" of computer science by researchers in academia, research institutions, and industry. Progress toward this goal has been pursued laboriously by a great number of distinguished colleagues and acquaintances since 1955, when the term Artificial Intelligence (AI) was coined. This goal of a truly autonomous system, capable of human-like thinking, contemplation, learning, making rational decisions, and acting on them has not been achieved to date. The reasons for the failure to achieve autonomy in a man-made system will become clear in this book; essentially, this failure is due to the need of a long-overdue paradigm shift in computer science.

The fundamental science referred to in the term "computer science" is not the science of computability; it is not the science of programmability; nor is it the science of abstraction, or of modeling, or of analysis, or of data processing.

The fundamental science in "computer science" is the *science of thinking*. And the fundamental product of computer science, *software*, is an abstraction of the human thought system. Without the full and complete understanding of these two fundamental ideas, an autonomous system can never become a reality.

ORIGINATION OF THE IDEA

Certainly the past efforts expended by our colleagues in Artificial Intelligence require appreciation and recognition. Their efforts are, to use a military analogy, as important as a route reconnaissance that has found that the area reconnoitered was not passable. This intelligence is as important to a field commander as finding the correct avenue of approach to the key terrain.

The other important recognition is for the paradigm shift in thought that came about by an open challenge in 1991 to the Jet Propulsion Laboratory's science and engineering divisions by its new director, Dr. Edward Stone. Before he became director, Dr. Stone was chief scientist of the Voyager Project at JPL, and our colleague. Upon his promotion, one of the first requests he made of the employees of our laboratory was to "think outside the box" and come up with a "paradigm shift" for JPL. This serious request inspired the thought process in the minds of several JPL employees. They developed a rational, well-developed concept for the architectural design of an autonomous system.

As the idea evolved under stress into a concept, it became clear that it was an achievable system. The realization that an autonomous system could be achieved came about through the intense thought exercises described by Immanuel Kant, Georg Wilhelm Friedrich Hegel, and Arthur Schopenhauer in their masterworks. Surprisingly, the architecture for the autonomous system is implied in their works in sufficient detail to be inferentially defined and articulated. Thus, the architecture presented in this book is the result of the paradigm shift requested by Dr. Stone. The system's fully functional cognitive attribute is purely software—the *mind* of the autonomous system.

That the mind is mathematically very intense may be intimidating at first glance. However, this will pose no problems that cannot be resolved with the appropriate mathematical tools. Hegel in his *Wissenschaft der Logik* points the way by his discourse on dynamic logic and quantum using integral and differential calculus.[2] The other essential mathematical tools needed for implementing complex operations and functions are readily available in Gradstein and Ryshik's beautifully compiled *Tafeln: Tables of Series, Products, and Integrals*.[3] This book has been a sheer delight to the mathematicians we know.

Hierarchical-sequential binary logic using algebra is a part of the mathematics of the architecture of the Thought system. However, Boolean logic[4] is only a part of the overall mathematics that form the operation of the human thought system; *it alone cannot lead to an autonomous system*. An autonomous system is no simple system; in fact, it is not a single system. A thinking machine capable of making rational decisions using the human mind as the model requires most of the equations listed in Gradstein and Ryshik.

THE NEGATIVE ASPECTS OF AN AUTONOMOUS SYSTEM

We must use caution here because we are dealing with a design object that will become a reality. There arises a serious question of ethics, reflecting whether we should build it or not. Consider: Does the design team require the autonomous system to be honest in its dealings with those who designed, built, and programmed it? Should it be obedient and forthright with the entire design team, or only with the architect or project manager? Should it be obedient to all instructions and commands received therefrom? This issue of forthrightness with the senior engineer or project manager is very important. Deciding who the single point of responsibility is for the design, implementation, fabrication, assembly, and testing of the autonomous system will play a crucial role.

This question is a valid and important issue and must be decided after careful consideration by the design team and by the sponsoring authority long before implementation begins. We, the human designers and builders, must determine if we want the autonomous system to be truthful and not have hidden agendas the way human beings do, fueled by omissions or outright falsehoods.

We must keep in mind also that an autonomous system initially will be, by design, either deterministic or nondeterministic. It will, from the point of initialization and actuation, be programmed in its intelligence to reflect the mental capacity of the finest human minds in academic and professional vocations. It will therefore begin to learn and gain experience with an IQ many times higher than ours without the hindrance of a *tabula rasa* to overcome. Thus, in the functional analysis and design, we are dealing in the first instance with *thinking*. An autonomous system must be able to think and to be self-aware. This too is a bridge between classical philosophy and modern computer science.

The negative aspects posed by a man-made, autonomous system could easily outweigh the benefits it may give humanity; hence, in this incarnation, it is designed to be deterministic, at least initially, and the application envisioned for it is oriented to interplanetary or interstellar exploration. Thus, the writing of this book and the contemplation of all that it implies must contain not only the architecture of the autonomous system, but relevant information bearing on the subject. As will become clear, the material must be presented in a format usable for the follow-up work in the design process and the development of a Class A spacecraft software system. In this instance, it is similar to the document format referred to as the Concept of Operations (CONOPS), which describes what a system must be able to do in support of its mission objectives.

The "holy grail" of computer science is not a "mere" autonomous system; it is a man-made system capable of thinking rationally, capable of learning everything the brightest among us can. It is capable of contemplation, making sound decisions, and acting on those decisions— on its own, without human intervention. The autonomous system is presented here as an achievable design object, and technically within our reach.

THE DIFFICULTY OF THE UNDERTAKING

The actual construction of an autonomous system is not a trivial matter, as the architecture outlined in this book will show. It cannot be built by an individual or even by a small, expert team of computer scientists. It can only be achieved as a large-scale project, the complexity and size of which will exceed the Voyager, Galileo, and Cassini flight projects combined and all the general and direct support systems they require, to use military terms. Such general and direct support systems include navigation, tracking, and sequencing.

Much thought has gone into this concept since the Voyager spacecraft encountered Jupiter in 1979–1980. It is certainly an achievable goal within the framework of the mental energy, work discipline, intellectual depth, creativity, and the engineering and science experience present at JPL during the era of the great spacecraft flight pioneering projects. During those days, only JPL and its superb minds were able to do it. Today, space exploration is still challenging, but is gradually transitioning to become more of a commodity, with numerous ready launch vehicles to choose from, and more on the way.

POINTS OF DEPARTURE

There are a number of ideas that have evolved into solid concepts that serve as the cornerstones for the architecture presented in this book. The first point of departure is the idea that computer software is an abstraction of the human thought system.[5]

The second and immediate point of departure is based on the famous dictum of René Descartes: "*Cogito, ergo sum*"—I think, therefore I am. Immanuel Kant went one better on this theme by stating: "*Cogito, ergo est*"—I think, therefore *it is*. These Latin *dicta* have many important implications to the computer scientist who is concerned with building an autonomous system. As mentioned earlier, any truly autonomous system, whether it be deterministic or nondeterministic, must by definition be able to think and be self-aware. The property of self-awareness means being able to think utilizing the attribute of self and nonself-discrimination. Therefore, *a machine is considered autonomous only when it can think, contemplate, speculate, and make rational decisions on its own without human intervention*. An autonomous machine must be able to think and act on its own, like an intelligent human being—an average human mind will not suffice. Thus, the only functional model we can use for such an autonomous cognitive capability is the *human* mind—the mind, not the brain. It is the mind we must use as the model for the design.

The principal question therefore is: What is the human thought system? No one has seriously attacked this problem since Immanuel Kant in 1792, Georg Wilhelm Friedrich Hegel in 1820, and Arthur Schopenhauer in 1830. Kant began this line of inquiry by conducting what he termed *Gedankenexperimente*—thought experiments—in the classrooms of the university where he taught, the University of Königsberg, known today as Kaliningrad, located in the former Kingdom of Prussia.

The third point of departure concerns the process of selecting the architectural model to be used for the cognitive component of the autonomous system. The only practical model for this is described in the collective works of Kant, Hegel, and Schopenhauer. When reading the works of these philosophers, one must be able to imagine or visualize the model of the mind presented therein, for if an engineer cannot imagine in detail the object to be designed, he or she cannot design it, much less build it. Considering the construction of this model from the viewpoint of modern computer science, it should be clear that the computer hardware equivalent in the human being is the brain. The computer software equivalent is the human mind, for it is the mind—not the physical structure of the brain—that comprises the various operating systems, processes, and suites of applications software, although the physical structures of the human brain are designed to support the functions it executes. So it is with the autonomous system.

THE SCOPE OF THIS BOOK

We have chosen an interplanetary/interstellar spacecraft as the implementation design object of a deterministic autonomous system. The reasons for this are relatively straightforward. The first is the familiarity of the authors with very large spacecraft systems. The second is that a system capable of flying an interstellar mission successfully must be able to do what a human being can do, or better. The third is to isolate a potentially unlimited system from us and our environment.

This book provides sufficient design detail to be presented to a project, and details how the design fits into an overall architecture for implementation. Any greater detail than what we present here would make this book too large to be manageable by a design team. This book, therefore, is the bridge between the Idea and the Concept for the Functional Design (FDD) and Functional Requirements (FRD) documents. More precisely, this is the Concept of Operations for the autonomous system, without which it would be impossible to accomplish.

SZABOLCS MICHAEL DE GYURKY
MARK A. TARBELL

Introduction

ARCHITECTURAL DESIGN OF THE AUTONOMOUS SYSTEM

This book is neither theoretical nor algorithmic; this is a book of *design*. We restrict ourselves to the preproject design phase of a cognitive software architecture of a true autonomous system. Because of the huge scope of the material, care must be taken not to wander off the ordered path to the goal, which is the implementation of the design object. The design object is the mind of the autonomous system, which is modeled on the human mind, the computer software equivalent. This principal issue of differentiation between the brain (hardware) and the mind (software) is but the first point of departure from the architecture of most artificial intelligence software. The software architecture of the mind—in the case of the autonomous system—includes the operating system software, the application software, the sensory interfaces, and data conversion processing software, compartmentalized into discrete entities known as *systems* in an overarching *constellation*.

THE OBJECTIVE

The first and most important issue of this book is that of presenting the architecture of the cognitive functions of an autonomous system in sufficient detail for an engineering team to begin the requirements and design process required for the building of the design object. This is the goal. The concept presented here therefore is not theoretical. This concept is firmly anchored in both philosophy and applied technology in Immanuel Kant's *Kritik der reinen Vernunft*. Kant's obsession with how human beings think was based on his love of Isaac Newton's *Philosophiae Naturalis Principia Mathematica* and the works of Wolff, Leibniz, Laplace, Shaftesbury, and the other giants of thought of his time, under the guidance of his mentor and professor, Martin Knutzen.

Note that this work is heavily influenced by classical cognitive philosophy. Nonetheless, one must keep in mind what changes in languages and their usage have done to the term "philosophy." The word originally meant "science and knowledge." Take for example the era in which Arthur Schopenhauer worked and wrote. He translated the title of Sir Isaac Newton's masterpiece into 19th-century German as *Naturwissenschaft, Mathematische Prinzipien*, which in today's English translates as "Natural Sciences: The Principles of Mathematics." So when we are discussing *Philosophiae Naturalis*—"the philosophy of nature"—we are discussing natural science.

To design and build the design object as a formal project is certainly achievable. What will be difficult to build is the organization of the design/project team and to enforce the strict discipline required to adhere—to the letter—to a mature software management standard. For our purposes, the software management standard chosen as the most practical is JPL-STD-D-4000,[1] because of the application for which it was designed—space flight projects—and our familiarity with it. It is a mature product and has repeatedly proven its value for controlling the design process and keeping the cost low and economically efficient, and the development time unfailingly on schedule.[2]

With respect to the presentation of this material, there were a number of important approaches that had to be followed in its scope and format. The foremost of these concerns the compromise between the styles used in writing a textbook and the writing of a design document. The former is a book from which to teach a subject; the latter is a technical document conveying engineering design material to be built or fabricated. The skills required for writing the Functional Requirements Document (FRD) or Functional Design Document (FDD) for a large and complex system differ from those used to teach in a classroom. The material in an FRD or FDD is formulated not to teach but to describe in detail what is to be built to individuals who are already accomplished scientists or software engineering professionals. The process of integrating the two styles is critical in computer software. The FRD is the first volume of many in the discipline of a serious software management standard. Especially in software engineering, we are dealing with human language, the understanding of and command of which may vary significantly between individuals, even among native speakers. Without a flawlessly articulated FRD, which is the result of synthesizing huge amounts of material represented by the volumes of important and very relevant reference works, the other design documents will be flawed and useless. Thus, human language in computer science plays a critical role, and the problems stemming from languages are usually manifested in the excessive overall cost of software, schedule slips in delivery, and high failure rates.

THE DISCOVERY PROCESS

It is important that the reader be made familiar with the historical sequence of events as they occurred and led to the definition of the architecture of the autonomous system. These are important events of human perception, insight, and understanding, acquired through reading and listening to design presentations and reviews during mission planning phases and mission operations. The abstract information is synthesized into knowledge through hands-on work and participation in the design and operations processes.

The discovery process forms the logical baseline of thought. Without a thorough understanding of how we think and learn and its importance to modern computer science, the software engineering and science associated with true autonomy is not possible. To begin with, it must be noted that without the works of the great cognitive philosophers, in particular Kant, Hegel, and Schopenhauer, the implementation of the architecture presented here would not have been possible. The impact of these great philosopher-scientists on the autonomous system will become very clear as one progresses through this book. The works of Immanuel Kant—specifically the three "Critiques": *The Critique of Pure Reason, The Critique of Practical Reason*, and *The Critique of Decision and Judgment*—form an inseparable part of the foundation of the autonomous system. These are followed by Arthur Schopenhauer's *The World as Will and Presentation*, and finally G.F.W. Hegel's *The Science of Logic* and *The Science of Being*.[3]

One must also accept the unenviable task of reading through such daunting works as Kant's *Critique of Pure Reason*, which is an absolute must because it stands by itself in cognitive philosophical achievement. The reason is best described by Professor August Messer, who published a reprint of the *Critique of Pure Reason* circa 1924.[4]

Kant's singular place in the development of our philosophical thinking is based in this, that it was he who took on the old schools of opposing philosophical positions: Naturalism, Idealism, Empiricism, and Rationalism in a wide and deeply thought-out Synthesis of reconciliation. Far from all prejudices, and preferences, he invites these opposite and contentious parties as equals before the seat of judgment of his "critical philosophy." He examines without taking side or partisanship the correctness or incorrectness of their positions and arrives at the results that they are not bounded by irreconcilable differences, but that there is a higher Entity which can reconcile all sides.

The works of the nineteenth-century scientist-philosophers and thinkers are much more serious and relevant than we had anticipated. In the prologue of Arthur Schopenhauer's book, *The World as Will and Presentation*, the requirements he sets are as true today as they were in his day. He says without hesitation or qualification:

You cannot read my books without being completely versed in Immanuel Kant's Critiques. *I'm a Kantian scholar. Furthermore, you cannot read my work,* The World as Will and Presentation, *only once. You must read it thoroughly twice. Once for familiarization, and then to mark it up and study it!*[5]

Schopenhauer was absolutely correct in this: One must read these works numerous times to connect them professionally to modern computer science. This process requires years of discipline, commitment, repetition, and practice. With this effort comes the benefit of expanding one's mind, forcing the brain to support and accommodate the mind's work to be able to view and process the monumental works from the perspective of an engineer, a computer scientist, or an architect, instead of as a student of philosophy. The modern computer scientist will learn the important things hidden in these texts that have been ignored by contemporary scholars. The ignorance of these treasured discoveries is due mainly to the fact that these books have been treated as "mere philosophy" and not as a part of science and engineering. It is the discovery of important vignettes of information that forces one to read every line.

The newly embraced empirical sciences, such as physics, biology, and chemistry, separated themselves a few hundred years ago from the metaphysical sciences, such as speculative logic and ontology.

Objective logic then took the place of these sciences.[6] As one reads through these works while working on spacecraft systems software, the relationship between modern 21st-century computer science and classical cognitive philosophy is startling and yet totally reasonable.

HUMAN LANGUAGE IN DESIGN

In this book, we place emphasis on the importance of languages in communication, both verbal and written. Simple and small languages do not lend themselves to great achievements, be it in art, science, or engineering. Neither do small languages broaden the minds of its thinkers. A large, complex language, when coupled to a well-disciplined education, should generally indicate a large, developed mind. Certainly there are exceptions due, say, to the laziness of the possessors or their own lack of experience. In software design, this is important for the purpose of visualizing the brain and the mind with its systems.

Concerning the issue of languages, we find that during the period in which philosopher-scientists were teaching and writing, a dramatic change was taking place in linguistics. Until this time, almost all books in science and engineering (in fact, all serious books in science, engineering, law, and history) were written in Latin or Greek. Isaac Newton wrote primarily in Latin. The reason for this is clear. Latin[7] was far superior to all the languages of its day except perhaps Greek. Latin and Greek are precise, unambiguous languages; these were the languages in which all important documents were written, regardless of whether the author was English, French, German, or Dutch. For serious scholars, it was enough to know one's mother tongue plus Latin and Greek. It was not necessary to learn German, French, English, or Russian. Isaac Newton and Immanuel Kant could therefore read and do research in the original texts written by Galen in medicine, Procopius in civil history, or Aristotle in science and philosophy. In all sciences, this was important and saved much time and effort. With the spread of the Roman Empire, the great schools and universities went wherever the borders of the Empire were, like Trier in Germany, and Lyons in France. The Moslem conquest of Constantinople and the submission of the professors to Islam gave the conquerors quite an advantage in science and engineering, for while

Europe languished in the Dark Ages after the collapse of the Empire in the West, Constantinople and the Empire in the East remained a cultural haven, with great universities, manufacturing, and commercial centers along with banking and trade. Even after the Empire in the West fell with Rome, and the new Western kingdoms were established, the Roman emperor in the East, Constantinople, continued to subsidize the universities and monasteries in the West even if these were Roman Catholic as opposed to Greek Orthodox. These subsidies kept the Latin and Greek languages current for scholarship[8] throughout the former Empire in the West.

The trend toward using national languages began at about the time of Isaac Newton's death. Schopenhauer complains[9] about this trend because none of the national languages, including the German, French, and English of his day, was suitable for serious science and engineering.

At that time, German scholars and scientists, being serious and anticipating an explosion in science, engineering, and the arts, decided to reconstruct the German language for the future; whether they coordinated in the effort or did it individually is unknown to the authors. The transition from Latin and Greek to German becomes evident from the difficulty of reading the classical German language of the original texts. There are many Latin and Greek words used, and the grammar and sentence structure becomes complex. This is true of the English language also. The transition to making German a great tool for science, engineering, medicine, and law took a long time, as evidenced by the writings. Very often, when Schopenhauer found that the translation of an idea or concept became too complicated or lost much of its meaning, he simply wrote it in Greek or Latin or at times in English. The sentences of Kant are often 150 words or longer. When reading Kant as a software architect, one finds the terms he uses are different in their philosophical expression compared with those used by Schopenhauer and his generation—not to mention the terms we use in modern computer science. Kant uses for example the term "islands in a sea" when describing the subsystems of the "Pure Understanding."[10]

The creative interpretation of these "islands" is accomplished as Euler spheres connected by Lambert lines to show relationships of the systems in time and space,[11] represented as the Phenomenon (information/data from, through, and by the senses) and the Noumenon (a thing unto itself, independent of external sensory or intellectual perception of it. Its root is from the Greek word *nouein*, which means to conceive or apprehend in the mind). We used this to great success in the computer systems architecture of the Global Decision Support System[12] instead of other traditional techniques because of severe schedule and budget constraints.

The modern computer scientist with a PhD in computer science has a definite advantage in dealing with the issue of modern and classical languages, whereas those with a BS or MS degree without a rigorous grounding in German, Latin, or Greek will be at a disadvantage at first. It is important to always keep in mind that we are not dealing in philosophy *per se*, but in a new computer science, a cognitive one.

The importance of the experience gained through participation and observation in, for example, the authors' major projects at the Jet Propulsion Laboratory (JPL), cannot be ignored or discounted. The part played by the use and application of science, engineering, and software development and management standards puts these on an equal footing with the other constructs. It was on the Voyager Project that advancements in spacecraft engineering, physics/astrophysics, human organization, navigation, sequencing, planning, and technology, with the brilliant minds of the principal investigators and project staff, made the project successful.

Today, computer science engineering technology has arrived at a maturation point: memory is cheap, fast, dense, small, and light; CPU/GPU architectures are efficient, massively multipipelined, multicored, hyperthreaded, scalable, and virtualized; and architectural design knowledge—based on the aforementioned constructs—has developed to once more make a giant leap possible: a thinking, learning, contemplative machine capable of rational thought and decisions, with the ability to communicate internally and externally in a human language.

OBSERVATION IN DESIGN

Let us consider by means of an analogy something as weighty as experience gained through observation and participation, which will be discussed repetitively throughout this volume because it is absolutely relevant. There is a commentary on analogy in Plato's Republic by

Socrates, which is as true today as it was during his lifetime, so we would like to quote it in full.

Adimantus is speaking:

> *"But what analogy do you perceive, Socrates, in the inquiry about justice?"*
>
> *"I will tell you, said I: do we not say that justice affects an individual man and an entire state also?"*
>
> *"Certainly," replied he.*
>
> *"Is not a state a greater object than an individual?"*
>
> *"Greater," said he.*
>
> *"Perhaps then, justice will be more fully developed in what is greater, and also more intelligible: we will first, then, if you please, inquire what it is in states; and then, we will in like manner examine it in the individual, searching for the similitude of the greater in the idea of the less."*[13]

Learning how human beings think, interact, solve problems, make decisions, select solutions, and communicate opinions or positions, taken in the environment of an interplanetary space flight mission, is subject to the same rules, with somewhat different objectives. The overall project organization of the Voyager Project, with its offices, teams, and procedures used to communicate decisions, requests, and opinions, is simply the equivalent of the "state" (greater) as discussed by Socrates, and the scientist or engineer is the equivalent of the "individual" (lesser).

During 1970–2000, the major flight projects of JPL represented the height of human development in science and engineering teamwork. Considering the individuals participating in these magnificent flight projects—the scientists, engineers, manager-architects, and programmers—the level of individual knowledge, sophistication, creativity, discipline, and experience on display was an amazing spectacle. To participate and to observe the interaction, planning, decision-making, and unqualified adherence to objective reality and truth by the project members was impressive.

THE PRESENTATION IN DESIGN

In considering the power of the Presentation part of the mind as elaborated by Kant, Hegel, and Schopenhauer, it becomes clear that the

Presentation is today either taken for granted and not given sufficient credit, or is absent in most human beings. In German, it is called *Vorstellung*, or idea/presentation. This word and concept, function and process, had to be separated from the Reason for modern architectural reasons as will be clarified later. However, *Vorstellung* means that it includes the *Anschauung*, which is the viewing of ideas, objects, concepts, sounds, smells, vibrations, and temperatures projected by the mind—in short, everything a human being is capable of thinking or contemplating. So it is when reading requirements or listening to the elaborations of a proposal, a concept, or an idea. This is the most startling discovery of the initial *Anschauung* or mental visualization of the human mind based on Kant's *Kritik der reinen Vernunft* and the relationship between the Phenomenon and Noumenon[14] architecturally.

In the human being, "rational thinking" as an attribute is not a given. The ability to think rationally is an acquired attribute; it requires much practice and discipline, hence Hegel's conclusion that the process of thinking can be devoid of all substance. Consider the human thought system as a network. This network may be utilized heavily, partially, or not at all from an engineering point of view, without processing data of any significance beyond the Will's drive for survival, reproduction, and dominance (e.g., a purely animalistic, biological driver).

LOGIC, MATHEMATICS, AND BIOLOGY IN DESIGN

During several decades of designing and building computer software for spacecraft missions, and participating in the daily, sometimes hourly, design team meetings, great insights were gained, which benefitted the consideration of how an autonomous system would work. A space flight project like Voyager is a showplace of the sciences, engineering, and mathematics, in the form of human expertise on a global scale. The interaction of principal investigators, team chiefs, and scientists is highly instructive to the participants and to observers seeking to accomplish a science mission. They must cooperate regardless of personal preferences, egos, or status in the hierarchy, because their failure to cooperate for the common goal will lose the prize, which is the accomplishment of the science mission. All meetings, action items, and tasks are an absolute necessity. There is no time to waste because, especially during critical periods, such as the closest approach to a planet like Jupiter, the science experiments demand absolute efficiency in the operation of the spacecraft, the scheduling of the antennae around the world, and the availability of the network for the reception of telemetry and the uplinking of commands. This can happen efficiently, not only by meticulous planning and execution, but also by making emergency corrections to the software and hardware due to anomalies in the encounter sequence caused by unforeseen events, all without losing time on the experiments of the instruments. How human beings accomplish this (or fail to) as a group is nothing more than a Socratic state—the "greater" representation of the thought processes, decision mechanisms, and problem-solving abilities of the "lesser," which is the individual, all of which is observable as in a motion picture theater or laboratory. In Hegel's philosophy, this process is called *Intellektuelles Anschauung*, or intellectual observation. The inference of the synthesis is, of course, logic.

The most readily acceptable concept of logic is to think of logic as pure thought. We then postulate as Hegel and Kant did that logic is the *science of pure thinking*,[15] where the translation here is not so much "pure" as in uncorrupted thinking, but rather thought uncluttered by ignorance, prejudice, preferences, or thinking in a language unsuitable or not sufficiently advanced for serious logical and scientific thought. The process of thought and deliberation both in their transcendental and visible forms or manifestations is very much representable in mathematical equations.

These terms were at first not obvious to us, but in the heat of group discussion and intense deliberation during the occultation phase of the Voyager spacecraft at Jupiter, they became clear. Hegel's lengthy discourse on the quantum[16] and his postulate that the quantum is best understood by using tools such as differential calculus aroused attention. Fortunately, the major equations from Newton and Leibnitz, from Euler to Lagrange, have been beautifully compiled[17] in both German and English, as translated from the original Russian.

Finally, there is the issue of biology to consider. We address the human thought system as the model for the autonomous system. Since all living things, whether plant or animal, are fundamentally biological, their behavior will be reflected in this journey from an idea through this concept and transition to the design of a thinking, learning, and acting system capable of making rational decisions without human intervention. It is for this reason that we have combined logic, mathematics, and biology here. All of these constructs play a role in the systems covered in this volume.

DESIGN ARTICULATION

More generally known as "documentation," *design articulation* is specified by software management standards. Several standards were consolidated in 1990 and renamed JPL-STD-D-4000, for use in the development of the Telemetry, Command, and Communication system (TCCS) project and the Operator/User Interface of the Ocean Topographic Explorer (TOPEX) project, Poseidon. After the launch of the spacecraft, JPL conducted an independent study to evaluate the benefits of using a software management standard.

The summary of their findings is as follows: TOPEX cost per line of code: $27.50. The average cost at NASA and industry at the time: $1200.00 per line of code.[18]

The technical content, clarity, organization, and completeness of expression in a FRD and all other documentation down to the Test Plan and Operator's Manual greatly impact the success or failure of a project, especially regarding schedule and cost. The FRD and FDD of the proposed design object may be poorly written, making them difficult to accept, both by academics and other persons unfamiliar with the design and construction of engineering items, because of the sheer discipline and scope of work required.

Ultimately, it is the system manager-architect's[19] responsibility to ensure the completeness of the architectural design. The method of arriving at an "acceptable reality"[20] in a design object is such that one takes the stated and clearly identified functional systems and completes the architecture by identifying and adding the implied design objects that have been left unstated. Often, after the implied functional requirements have been included in the architecture, numerous derived functional requirement capabilities are discovered. These derived requirements are then added to the architecture of the design object, making the overall design clean and understandable, giving the architecture sufficient or acceptable reality. The term "acceptable reality" means that a system (or design object larger than a system) is ready for implementation.

Without the application of a rigorous, disciplined engineering process as encapsulated in a software management standard, a project becomes prohibitively expensive. Therefore, the failure referred to as "creeping requirements"[21] cannot be tolerated in a highly complex and large design object. All functional requirements must be identified, beginning with the stated requirements, then on to the implied requirements, and finally to the derived requirements. Flawless technical English must be maintained throughout.

Language therefore plays a crucially important role in implementation. Language is very important in that human beings think in languages; the level of our understanding of a particular problem depends not only on the size and flexibility of the languages we think in, but also in how we communicate the problems and solutions with others.

CHAPTER 1

The Architecture of the Autonomous System

A system of thoughts must always have an architectural structure.

—Arthur Schopenhauer, *Die Welt als Wille und Vorstellung*[1]

1.1 INTRODUCTION

The main objective of this chapter is to introduce the architecture of an autonomous system. This requires several clarifications, in that the architecture is not presented as an hypothesis or theoretical work, but as a design object to be built. It is therefore presented in the spirit, fashion, and format as commonly done in the preproject phase of a proposed mission or project.

1.2 THE SYSTEM CONSTELLATION

It was our original intention to provide a Level II description of the software architecture. However, it became very clear that from a computer science software architectural perspective, the mind is not a single system but a "system of systems," better described collectively as a *constellation*. Nor can such an enormously large object as the human

The Autonomous System: A Foundational Synthesis of the Sciences of the Mind, First Edition. Szabolcs Michael de Gyurky and Mark A. Tarbell.

mind be implemented as single system with a number of subsystems. Such an undertaking would be exceedingly difficult to design because the interfaces and subsystems would become too numerous, too complicated, too difficult to identify for design purposes, and overlapping/intertwined in that some are separate systems and others are functions and processes that permeate numerous systems.

During the period in which the *Critiques* et al. were written, German as a language was in a state of change, and the various authors, although thinking in terms of systems (σύστημα or *sustēma* in Greek), had no idea of the distant development of computer science and its potential as a tool for replicating human functions. The object, therefore, is not a single system with dedicated subsystems, but a constellation of nearly independent, unique entities or systems. Onward, we will call this replication of the human mind the *system constellation*. Thus, the architectural design will need to be presented at Level I. This will apply to the overview of the system constellation as a whole, as well as to each of the systems within the constellation presented in the chapters to follow. For a design team to flesh out and complete this architecture at the lower implementation levels, there must be a clear starting point for a disciplined systems approach to begin, or the goal will never be reached.

Note that even though the emphasis herein is necessarily on the software (mind) domain of the systems architecture, care must be taken not to forget about the hardware (brain and sensory) domain. Being mindful of the hardware required to support the software design helps to put the entire system constellation into proper and understandable context and perspective. This will also help to ensure a realizable system when the time comes for implementation. After all, it is the hardware and sensors that provide the processing capacity and communications connectivity of the system constellation. Nevertheless, the hardware design portion comes only after a complete software architecture has been designed, for it is the hardware design that supports the software design, not the other way around. This process is one of visualization—it was Hegel's quantum that offered the first doors of visualization into the architecture of the mind and the relationship it had to the brain. The architecture of the brain is based on the information processing requirements of the mind and—as is true in any flight project—the associated communications and sensory requirements.

1.3 SYSTEM CONSTELLATION ARCHITECTURAL OVERVIEW

There are in the human brain two separate but linked hemispheres. The two hemispheres have similar architectures or anatomies, and for the sake of this design, they are treated as equal. The conclusions of Arthur Schopenhauer reveal a very intriguing phenomenon. He states that the *Idea*[2] (i.e., pure reason, not based on empirical experience) in a thought process originates from that part of the mind dedicated to the arts, such as music, poetry, and art. The *Concept*[3] (i.e., empirically derived understanding) in a thought process, however, originates from that part of the mind dedicated to science and engineering.

Thus, at the time he was making this observation, Schopenhauer established that the right hemisphere tended to support artistic thought, and the left hemisphere tended more to scientific and engineering-oriented thought.[4] This is important in the design of an autonomous system in that such a system must be able to take a thought process from the Idea to the Concept. In human beings, where the two hemispheres are tightly coupled, this arrangement lends itself to a tremendously powerful capacity for thinking, problem-solving, contemplation, and decision. This is indeed true only of some human beings, not all. However, for the purposes of the autonomous system, we can view the left/right dichotomy of the human brain as an implementation detail, and one of biological expedience. Since in the human mind, the ideational systems (Reason, Presentation, and Understanding) generally interact among themselves more than they do with the conceptual systems across the divide (e.g., Will, Intellect, Sensory, and Decision), and vice versa, this tightly coupled arrangement would benefit their mutual interoperation. In the autonomous system, such a design may also prove to be useful should the processing requirements be so high that it becomes necessary or desirable to do so. (One must always keep in mind, however, that the elements of the design of the mind of the autonomous system such as this ultimately will be dependent on the requirements posed by the sponsor.)

There are certain ground rules for such a machine. One such rule is that it must have an image of *self*, that is, it will be conscious of *being*. Being, or being self-aware, means that it must be able to think and to contemplate. It must be able to receive instructions, learn, be receptive to instructions and orders, and carry them out. It must be able to make rational decisions without human input, and act upon those decisions. Finally, it must be able to communicate with man, with other autonomous systems of its kind, and also among its own internal systems in the *human language* it is given by design. Thus, it is imperative to acknowledge that language is far too important in an autonomous system to be glossed over. It pays a dominant role in the way we think, read, write, and communicate, listen, and understand. So it is with the autonomous system.

The functional capability for a man-made machine to be able to think is a very serious one. As will be seen in the architectural overview, *all of thinking is a function of communication (language) among the numerous systems of the constellation.*[5]

For ease of understanding, the architecture is presented in terms of acceptable reality.[6] The eight systems that comprise the autonomous system constellation are identified and defined according to the methodology attributed to traditional systems architecture and engineering practices. This approach will first identify those systems that have been addressed in detail in the form of functional requirements or functional descriptions. The systems that are stated, having been identified, are then followed by those systems that are implied by the stated functional requirements/description, keeping in mind that very often, functional requirements and functional descriptions are interchangeable.

Because we are looking at the masterworks of the great thinkers of the eighteenth century not from the perspective of contemporary students of philosophy, but as computer scientists, we have to read these works as functional requirements and functional designs. The first thing that we are confronted with is that the terms intelligence, presentation, reflection, understanding, reason, and so on are often used in different ways, as systems in themselves, or as processes or products. For the sake of a rationally designed system, the architecture must be inferred and the design put into logical and understandable form. Exactly where a function or process takes place is not nearly as important as its product and quality.

The last step in this process—identifying those functional requirements not explicitly stated or implied—is finished by identifying the derived functional requirements and descriptions. The systems that are derived are usually those that the architect or systems engineer feel are needed to make a system work properly, without interruption, and which are available to the user or designer on a virtual basis. In this category would fall, for example, redundant processing systems and the like.

1.4 THE CONSTELLATION ARCHITECTURE

Figure 1.1, Figure 1.2, and Figure 1.3 show three different depictions of the architecture of the system constellation. Figure 1.1 shows a simple line-art schematic of the basic entities in flat space. Figure 1.2 depicts a three-dimensional cutaway view of the constellation, showing the systems and how they embed in the Noumenon and Phenomenon regions. Figure 1.3 depicts an overhead 3D view of the constellation, showing the various systems and their arrangement.

In each of the figures, the outer sphere surrounding the systems of the constellation is the external communication network, the Phenomenon network. This network is the network of the senses, which

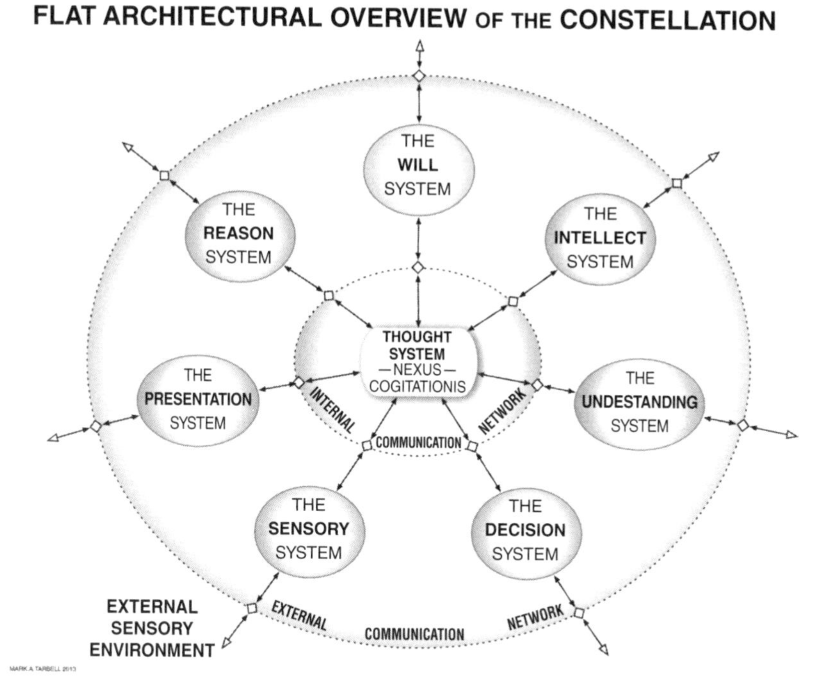

FIGURE 1.1 A 2D flat architectural overview of the autonomous system constellation, showing all systems and their relationships.

3D OCTANT ARCHITECTURAL VIEW OF THE CONSTELLATION

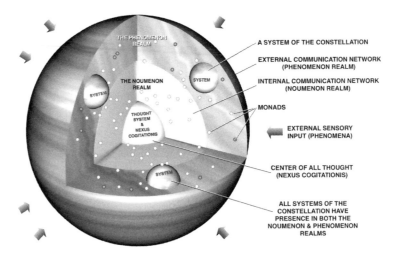

FIGURE 1.2 A 3D octant cutaway architectural view of the autonomous system constellation, showing the structure of the Noumenon and Phenomenon realms with respect to the systems embedded within.

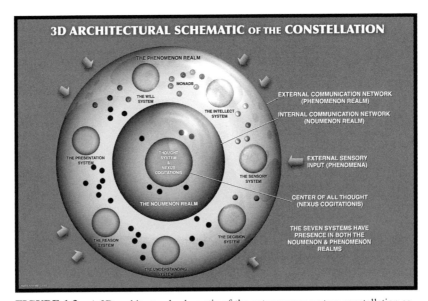

FIGURE 1.3 A 3D architectural schematic of the autonomous system constellation as viewed from the outside, showing all of the systems in the Noumenon and Phenomenon realms.

transmits all data perceptible to the senses, be they facts or occurrence. This high-speed network is the medium that brings into the system constellation all external sensory information. The information from the external sensors represents the varied phenomena of the environment in which the autonomous system exists, as well as the state of the phenomena of the mechanical state of the constellation itself. These Phenomenon data are carried by an uninterrupted and continuous flow of *monads*.[7] The phenomena are presented in the forms of sound, color, temperature, state (of motion), optical/spectral characteristics, and so on.

The next inner sphere represents the internal communication network, or Noumenon network, which transmits the intellectual (thought) perceptions and intuitions between the systems in a natural (human) language. The Thought system is supervised by the *Nexus Cogitationis*, the center of all thought. The Nexus is a necessary system inferred from the material presented by Kant, Hegel, and Schopenhauer in their works, not explicitly mentioned or discussed but implied out of architectural necessity. The Thought system is also orchestrated by the Nexus Cogitationis. This is the architectural network that facilitates the process of thought and gives the autonomous system a sense of being and consciousness, of self and existence. The Thought system is the internal network tightly coupled to all of the systems of the constellation, processing on the order of billions of monadic transactions per second. This enormous volume of data processing is based on dynamic logic in addition to the simpler hierarchical, sequential logic.[8]

1.4.1 The Four Categories of Communication

A brief overview of the four categories of communication transmissions is in order.[9]

(a) The *Monologue*, a one-way simplex transmission of any given system to another given system

(b) The *Dialogue*, a two-way duplex transmission between any two systems

(c) The *Broadcast*, a one-way simplex transmission by any one system to some or all of the systems

(d) The *Conference* transmission, a multiplexed *n*-to-*n* communication. This is a communication mode in which many or all of the systems of the constellation participate in problem-solving and consideration of courses of action to be developed to deal with a problem confronting the constellation as a whole. In human terms, this would be considered a discussion or debate.

The Nexus Cogitationis is the constellation's *Konzertmeister*, the communication controller, but also much more. It is here that the process of thinking begins,[10] where all thought activity is monitored, and at times, as with a very disciplined and intelligent human mind, where thinking is orchestrated. It is here that the functions of contemplation, consideration, and self-awareness/self-consciousness take place.

1.5 THE SOFTWARE SYSTEMS COMPRISING THE CONSTELLATION

1.5.1 The Will System

The Will system is a stated design requirement.[11] The Will system is, functionally, the "executive system" of the constellation. It is the driving force of the physical existence of the autonomous system. All living creatures have a Will.

The Will system is the primary system of the mind, and as such, it is dominant in the constellation. In the cognitive sciences, the Will is an object, even considered to be the "thing unto itself."[12]

The Will system is the survival system, including survival of the individual and of the species (accomplishment of the mission, reproduction). It is the system of self-repair of malfunctions and reprogramming, and the system of dominance (to rule, direct, decide, and dominate others of its species, including the other systems within the constellation). The Schopenhauerian concept is that the Will is an object, the "thing unto itself" that holds together all visible and nonvisible elements in a system. This makes logical sense from a software engineering point of view. If the Will system is an object to the architect, then so are the other systems in the constellation. This enables an understanding of the human thought process and allows for its modeling. Another reason for taking advantage of the concept of the "objectivization of the Will" is the famous dictum of Thucydides, "A compromise is only possible among equals; the powerful will ever extract tribute from the weak, while the weak will ever do the bidding of the strong."[13] In the intelligent and disciplined human mind, there is constant debate over the wanting to do something and the counter-argument of why not to do so. It therefore becomes clear to the systems architect that in the mind of an intelligent and disciplined human being, there are independent and objectivized systems as opposed to systems that simply go along with the dictates of the Will.

To the systems architect's advantage, this is a starting point for design. The Will system as an object is a stated design requirement in that it has been described and researched, dissected and discussed, fought and argued over by some of the finest scientific and mathematical minds in the world.

The primary subsystems of the Will system are the Environment subsystem, the Mission subsystem, the Executive subsystem, the Constellation Repair subsystem, and the Axioms subsystem, which acts as a database connected directly to the Reason system. See Figure 1.4.

The primary internal servers of the Will system are the Noumenon server, the Phenomenon server, and the Axioms server. All of the

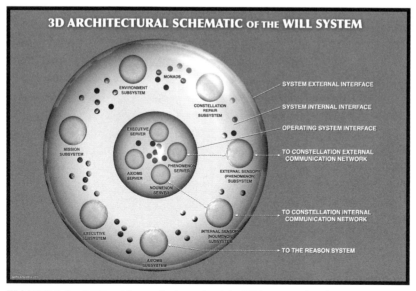

FIGURE 1.4 A 3D architectural schematic of the Will system, showing the internal servers and subsystems.

servers have extensive subfunctions. Consider from the architectural perspective the issue of the Axiom's[14] connection to the Reason system.

1.5.2 The Reason System

The Reason system is a stated requirement.[15] The Reason is described by Immanuel Kant as having two states. The first state is the Practical Reason,[16] and the second state is the Pure Reason.[17] In the functional architecture of the autonomous system's mind, the Reason system is the "conscience" of the mind. In the practical state, it participates not only in both routine and nonroutine operation of the constellation, but as an advisor albeit without executive powers. In the pure state, it is the leader of contemplation and reflection, pondering issues relating to everything important to the constellation.

It has three major subsystems or functional attributes. See Figure 1.5. The first attribute is the Laws subsystem, adherent to the unbreakable laws given by the systems architect or systems engineer to the autonomous system. The laws are the priorities for the protection of

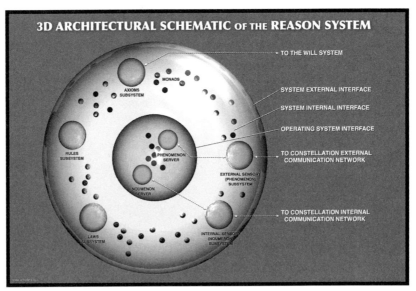

FIGURE 1.5   A 3D architectural schematic of the Reason system, showing the internal servers and subsystems.

the autonomous system and the environment in which it works. These laws are programmed into the constellation and are inviolable.

The second attribute is the Rules subsystem. Rules are not laws; they are guidelines for the effective and efficient operation of the autonomous system. Rules relate to working and learning, and may be modified through input from the other systems in the constellation or by external programming during the design phase of the autonomous system project.

The third attribute is the Axioms subsystem, which allows for a quick reference to summations of complicated rules, generally to avoid making a dangerous mistake.

Once the Reason system is properly programmed, there must be no conflict in the constellation as to following the rules, laws, and axioms for the accomplishment of the mission, especially between the Will system and the Reason system.

The Reason system has three servers: the Noumenon server, the Phenomenon server, and the Axioms server, which is a direct link to the Will system.

1.5.3 The Intellect System

The Intellect system is an implied system. It is addressed by Kant, Hegel, and Schopenhauer more like a function, a subsystem, or a process as opposed to an object of its own. However, it is an architectural necessity to have the Intellect as an object and system equal in standing to the other systems in the constellation, as it plays a critical role and performs the even more critical task of *intellection* in the autonomous system constellation. Intellection is the act or process of exercising the intellect through query and stimulation input, the capacity to acquire and apply knowledge. The Intellect system has the role of being the "librarian" of the autonomous system.

The Intellect system receives, processes, and stores all abstract data received through external sensory input. Abstract data are those data that human beings receive as second-hand information, such as from reading books, listening to lectures, reading technical papers, or observing from a distance. This type of data is often mistaken as "knowledge," but it is not. In human beings, this mistake almost always results in great catastrophe when one assumes that an individual who has mastered abstract data must therefore have knowledge. It is true that once

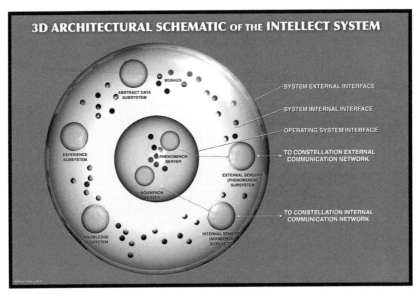

FIGURE 1.6   A 3D architectural schematic of the Intellect system, showing the internal servers and subsystems.

an individual has mastered abstract data, he can achieve a maximum score on an examination based on abstract information; however, unless the data have been validated by experience, the individual has no knowledge in the field. The processing of abstract data and its validation with experience is what results in knowledge.

In addition to the Noumenon and Phenomenon servers, the Intellect system has three major subsystems: the Abstract Data subsystem, the Experience subsystem, and the Knowledge subsystem. See Figure 1.6.

The Abstract Data subsystem acquires, processes, and stores all information gained from secondhand sources.

The Experience subsystem stores experiences in a database-like repository, be they good, bad, useful or not, harmful or beneficial. The abstract data are then validated by experience either in the field or in a laboratory. When the abstract data have been validated with contextual experience, they become knowledge. A sound decision is made first based on knowledge, then on experience, and only rarely on abstract data alone. When the Will system makes a calculated decision, it is based on the knowledge provided by the Intellect system and the rules provided by the Reason system.

The Knowledge subsystem processes abstract information and validates these through experience. This integration of real hands-on experience gained through trial and error to validate an abstract data set is the process of creating real knowledge. For our purposes in the design of an autonomous system and its cognitive functions, anything less than a perfect, correct, timely, and accurate decision is unacceptable. Even if the Will system is good and willing to accept and act on input from the Reason system (e.g., ethical rules, laws, and axioms), if the input from the Intellect system is based on incomplete information (e.g., primarily abstract knowledge), it follows that the decision will be flawed or wrong.

The main servers of the Intellect system are the Noumenon server and the Phenomenon server.

1.5.4 The Presentation System

The Presentation system is a stated and defined system.[18] The Presentation, as a system in the constellation, is the "theater of the mind."

The Presentation system is truly a virtual theater and a systems object with a phenomenal capability of displaying all sensations to the systems of the constellation. It is critically important to the survival of the autonomous system in that it can present the consequences of a decision made by the Will in real time. It has the capability of real-time presentation of one or more courses of action to anything under consideration by the constellation. The courses of action and their consequences, however, depend on the mode (contemplative vs. active) of the process, and include the following considerations:

- The completeness of the knowledge available from the Intellect system
- The rules, laws, and axioms provided by the Reason system
- The urgency of action for a decision, if in an active mode.

The presentation can be via any medium, such as sound, smell, temperature, motion, color, dimension, and size, and includes the sensations felt during a replay of experiences.

When dealing with the systems of the constellation, we are dealing with the mind of the autonomous system, and as such, the Presentation system is an objective system. The Presentation system is critical in that it can present the consequences of an action based on a decision made *a priori*. If the decision can have destructive consequences, it will play the entire motivation, action, and outcome instantly and thereby warn the autonomous system in the hope of changing the decision to a more positive course of action. If the Presentation is flawed, inhibited, or underdeveloped, it cannot perform as it does in a highly developed human mind.

The Presentation system also has a history database of all previous experiences, both pleasant and unpleasant, with all the surrounding facts bearing on the memory segment, and can replay all variations of the experience. This can manifest itself as contemplation, problem-solving, memory maintenance, or the preparation of sets of valid and invalid references.

In addition to the Noumenon and Phenomenon servers, the main subsystems of the Presentation system are the Viewing subsystem, the Projection subsystem, the Experience subsystem, the Analysis subsystem, the Recall subsystem, and the Contemplation subsystem. See Figure 1.7.

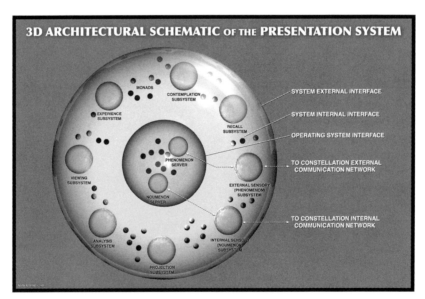

FIGURE 1.7 A 3D architectural schematic of the Presentation system, showing the internal servers and subsystems.

The servers of the Presentation system are the Noumenon server and the Phenomenon server.

1.5.5 The Understanding System

The Understanding system is inferred from the sum of the works used as reference in this book. It is in the Understanding system that the material for thinking is assembled, compiled, and presented to the constellation for review and consensus. See Figure 1.8. The German meaning of the word *Verständnis* includes not only understanding but the functional attributes of cleverness, recognition, and the ability to think clearly and concisely. This capability is missing in many human beings, manifesting itself in rather interesting ways, such as the running of red lights while driving. Thus, when contemplating the implementation process of building the autonomous system, it must be kept in mind by the design team that the Understanding system must not be permitted to make such mistakes. The autonomous system is to have *by design* a superior mind, with not only a well-developed Intellect, Reason, a

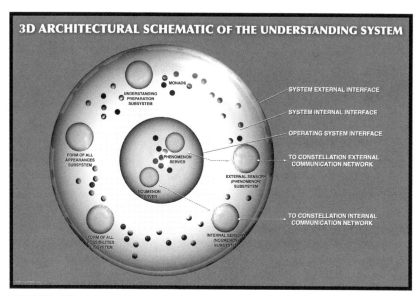

FIGURE 1.8   A 3D architectural schematic of the Understanding system, showing the internal servers and subsystems.

good Will, and a superb Presentation, but a full Understanding of what it must know to survive and to comprehend the mission objectives.

Some of the functional attributes of the Understanding system are the ability to learn (which is a capacity for applied knowledge), and the ability to process abstract data, experience data, as well as knowledge by accessing the Intellect system. Recall that *intellection* is the act or process of exercising the intellect through query and stimulation input; it is the very capacity to acquire and apply knowledge itself.

The main subsystems of the Understanding system are the Form of All Appearances subsystem, the Form of All Possibilities subsystem, and the Understanding Preparation subsystem. See Figure 1.8.

The main servers of the Understanding system are the Noumenon server and the Phenomenon server.

1.5.6 The Sensory System

The Sensory system is a stated and implied system. There can be no self-awareness or self-identity without external sensory information and an awareness of the external environment. This system, as with all of the systems of the constellation, is a design object, and as such, it is of equal standing with the other systems. It receives its external and internal sensory data by means of Phenomenon monads[19] from the sensors placed external to the autonomous system body. It receives the sensory input internal to the body from internal sensors, which monitor the electrical, mechanical, and scientific components and instruments through the Phenomenon monads also.

The subsystems of the Sensory system are the External Sensory (Phenomenon) subsystem, the Internal Sensory (Noumenon) subsystem, the Propulsion, Motion, and Manipulation subsystem, the Standards and Limits subsystem, and the Autonomous System State subsystem. See Figure 1.9.

The major servers of the Sensory system are the Noumenon server and the Phenomenon server.

1.5.7 The Decision System

The Decision system is a stated and defined system. This system is described both functionally and architecturally in great detail by Immanuel Kant.[20] It is both a system object as well as a complex architectural systems process. Ironically, from the perspective of Kant's

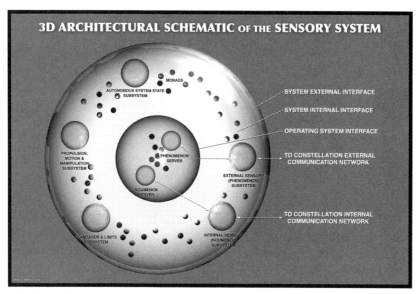

FIGURE 1.9 A 3D architectural schematic of the Sensory system, showing the internal servers and subsystems.

monumental work, modern computer-based "expert systems" and "decision systems" are so primitive as to be almost medieval. Modern decision systems are hierarchical and sequential, using little more than Boolean logic with a few algorithmic extensions. Kant's decision system utilizes *dynamic logic*, going beyond Aristotle.

The Decision system is therefore defined as a systems object of indispensable value. The German word *Urteilskraft* from the point of view of a systems architect and systems engineer has a broad meaning. *Urteil* in English means verdict, judgment, decision, view, and opinion; *Kraft* means strength, power, force, energy, efficacy, and validity. The Decision system therefore is not only the system where decisions are formulated and manufactured, but the system where the power and energy reside to *make* a decision, and a right one at that. For human beings, making a "correct" decision is not always the "right" decision. This is because the right decision is also dependent on ethical considerations.

As stated in the above, one functional aspect of making a decision is the energy and power required to do so. In human terms, especially in computer science software-intensive projects, we often encounter

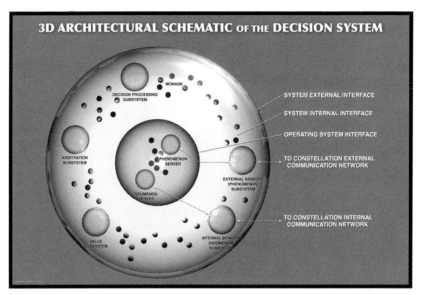

FIGURE 1.10   A 3D architectural schematic of the Decision system, showing the internal servers and subsystems.

people in engineering and management who "can't make a decision." From the perspective of an engineer on a project, if a manager or systems engineer can't make a decision, the consequences are terrible. Sometimes, spacecraft are lost or ships are sunk, all as a direct result of the inability to make a right decision.

Thus, the Decision system in the autonomous system constellation represents the "operations officer." It assembles all relevant data from the systems of the constellation and prepares a number of prioritized courses of action with the Will system.

The main subsystems of the Decision system are the Arbitration subsystem, the Value subsystem, and the Decision Processing subsystem. See Figure 1.10.

The major servers of the Decision system are the Noumenon server and the Presentation server.

1.5.8 The Thought System: Nexus Cogitationis

As a stated and defined system, and the ultimate object of the autonomous system constellation, the Thought system is the main purpose of this volume, that is, to explain how thinking works from a software architectural perspective. The Thought system is described as the internal communications of the autonomous system, showing the architecture of how the autonomous system will work once development starts.

The model used for the autonomous system is, of course, the *human* thought system. Indeed, there can be no other model for such a system because only human beings can describe and articulate how we think; only we as humans know *with understanding* how to drive an automobile or fly an aircraft. We also acknowledge that many of us as human beings cannot think or have otherwise impaired thought systems.

As a case in point, for the purposes of an autonomous system, we cannot model how a rat thinks because we cannot hold a conversation with a rat to discern more clearly how it processes data; we can only infer from observation.[21] This conscious inferential reasoning is unique only to a well-developed human mind. The idea of using the rat as the model for an autonomous system's cognitive process is not practical, since doing so would be based on empirical data only. The human mind is accessible through tests and dialogues held with those who have intelligent, well-developed minds.

This idea, now developed into a concept, has its origins in the thought experiments or *Gedankenexperimente* conducted by Immanuel Kant. An autonomous system that can exist on its own without human involvement must have a self-identity and a sense of being. G.F.W. Hegel addresses this in his work and experimental research.[22] A sense of being cannot exist without the consciousness of the existence of an external environment. This implies an ability to contemplate, reason, form judgments, make decisions, learn new things, act and do, and of course communicate with other intelligent beings. Thus, the Thought system must be simultaneously a stated, implied, and derived system object.

We are concerned here mainly with the functioning, operation, and structure of the thought process. Internal communication within the mind is carried by monads among the systems of the constellation in the form of thought-logic elements called *Noumena*, and the network of intellectual data flow operates in the forms of Monologue, Dialogue, Broadcast, and Conference transmission types. The human thought system is dynamic in character and is represented in the mathematical form of integral and differential calculus.[23] This is the dynamic logic of the mind, and it is Hegel who formalized it.

The Thought system is termed the *Nexus Cogitationis*, the center or hub of all thought. The Nexus Cogitationis monitors all of the channels of communication, including the Phenomenon (external communications), which requires its attention, and is involved when clarification is needed.

The Thought system contains within itself the primary communication engine of the autonomous system, for communication both within itself (among the systems) and with the world outside of the constellation. It can communicate in the human language it has learned through programming or on its own.

The Thought system serves as the central data distribution system between the systems of the constellation. It is an unlimited *n*-processor function itself, and can expand processor utilization/capacity on demand in accordance with the requirements and effort put into expansion in hardware and software, such as when the processing requirements of a particular system exceed the existing hardware and communications capability.

This expansion of the thinking power through the Thought system can be controlled and allocated according to the availability of processing space. Processing space in human beings for "rational thinking" can only be built through much effort, discipline, and practice. In short, it takes a willful determination and diligence to learn how to think in the human model. In the autonomous system, this capability is designed and programmed in by the design team.

All external and internal data communications are processed and monitored by the Thought system. Demands from sensors are received and passed on to the Sensory system and the Understanding system as a safeguard against missed sensor communications and commands.

In addition to the ubiquitous Noumenon and Phenomenon subsystems, the main subsystems of the Thought system are the Monologue subsystem, the Dialogue subsystem, the Broadcast subsystem, and the Conference subsystem. Each of these subsystems has its own corresponding server placed in the Nexus Cogitationis. The communication-related subsystems include the Fault Monitoring subsystem, the Command and Demand subsystem, and the Communication subsystem. See Figure 1.11.

The major servers of the Thought system are all communication-related: the Noumenon and Phenomenon servers, the Monologue and Dialogue subsystems, and the Broadcast and Conference servers. Note

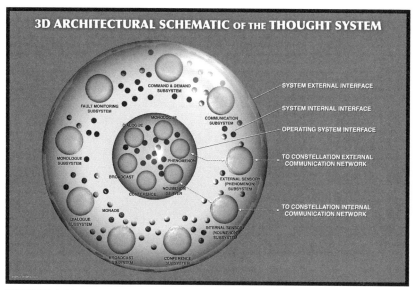

FIGURE 1.11   A 3D architectural schematic of the Thought system, showing the internal servers and subsystems.

that the Noumenon and Phenomenon servers drive "streaming networks" that flow steadily without stop-and-go. The internal information elements are carried and formulated as *Noumena*—thought fragments—by Noumenon monads, whereas the Phenomenon monads carry what is akin to sensual data in humans, and sensory data in mechanical devices.

CHAPTER 2

The Architectural Methodology

For want of a better word in the English language, the term *methodology* is used to best describe the mental process of the integration and synthesis of all physical materials available leading to the all-important starting point: the *Idea*. From the Idea, we arrive at the *Concept*.

The Idea is esteemed as a uniquely human attribute of the mind. Based on this *a priori* intuitive hypothesis,[1] we know:

(a) That a fully autonomous system can be built

(b) What its architecture will look like in software engineering terms

(c) What the scope of the work required will be to accomplish the implementation.

It is of great importance to understand the scope of such a project and the constraints that bind it, the prerequisites that accompany such an undertaking, and the discipline required for its achievement. The major constructs are computer science technology, large-scale software design, the cognitive dynamics of computer science, software implementation, testing, and documentation. The operations engineering and science skills required include flight mission analysis and planning, software testing and integration, user interface design, programming,

The Autonomous System: A Foundational Synthesis of the Sciences of the Mind, First Edition. Szabolcs Michael de Gyurky and Mark A. Tarbell.

and the application of software management standards. We will first proceed to outline the absolutely necessary discipline and development sequence to be followed in the design of the autonomous system, and then return to elaborate on the Idea and Concept.

2.1 ARTICULATION OF THE REQUIREMENTS AND DESIGN

For the sake of simplicity and manageability, we have broken down the entire articulation development process into descriptive phases, as depicted in Figure 2.1 and Figure 2.2, *The Development Cycle of The Autonomous System*, using a traditional "waterfall" approach, but allowing for iterative feedback between steps as needed.[2] The bottom line is that the architecture, design, and planning all must be *finalized* before the individual system implementation phases begin, else the design object will become an ever-moving target and ultimately unattainable. As a product, the autonomous system is not to be likened

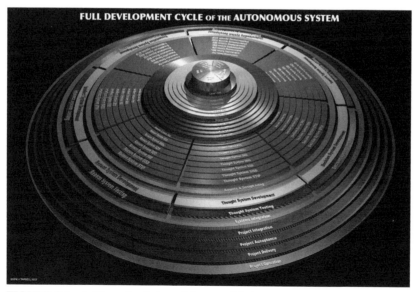

FIGURE 2.1   A 3D overhead view of the waterfall development cycle of the autonomous system. This figure provides an overview of the autonomous system constellation by presenting a breakdown of the software architecture of the constellation in Level I terms. Note the enormity of the undertaking, and that programming (white ring) comprises but 1 of the 28 levels.

FIGURE 2.2 A 3D close-up view of the waterfall development cycle of the requirements and design documentation portion highlighting the Thought system. Note that there are 21 levels that must be completed before system development can commence (outer white ring).

to a web-based application whose design changes daily according to user feedback or usage. It is a system whose first instantiation is designed to match the finalized point of *acceptable reality*; from thence the system will take itself where it chooses.

Figure 2.1 shows an overview of the development cycle of the entire autonomous system at a glance:

- Pillars of Knowledge and Experience
- Level I ADD: Project Architecture Design Document

- Project FRD: Project Functional Requirements Document
- Project FDD: Project Functional Design Document
- Project SRD: Project Software Requirements Document
- Project PIP: Project Implementation Plan
- Project PRC: Project Programming Rules and Conventions
- Project SDD: Project Software Design Document
- Project DDD: Project Detailed Design Document
- Project SSD: Project Software Specifications Document
- Project SISD: Project Software Interface Specifications Document
- Project STIP: Project Software Test and Integration Plan.

For each system in the Constellation:

- System FRD: Functional Requirements Document
- System FDD: Functional Design Document
- System SRD: Software Requirements Document
- System SDD: Software Design Document
- System DDD: Detailed Design Document
- System SSD: Software Specifications Document
- System SISD: Software Interface Specifications Document
- System STIP: Software Test and Integration Plan.

At the Constellation level:

- Systems Requirements and Design Integration.

At this point, the software articulation (documentation) is completed, finalized, and signed off. *Only after this has occurred may development begin:*

At the System Level
- System Development and Debugging
- System Testing.

At the Constellation Level
- Systems Integration Testing.

At the Project Level

- Project Integration Testing
- Project Final Acceptance Testing
- Project Delivery and Installation
- Project Operation and Maintenance.

2.1.1 Pillars of Knowledge and Experience

Starting at the center of Figure 2.2, there are the five equal foundational pillars of:

- **Immanuel Kant**. The Three Critiques
- **G.W.F. Hegel**. The Science of Logic/The Science of Being
- **Arthur Schopenhauer**. The World as Will and Presentation
- **JPL-STD-D-4000**. Software Management Standard
- **Real-World Large-Scale Project Experience**.

If any of these pillars is missing or lacking, project development cannot commence. The individuals chosen for the positions of system manager–architect, systems engineer, and the design team must be conversant at the expert level in all five pillars, or failure will ensue, for this expertise cannot be learned as "on-the-job" training.

2.1.2 Level I Architecture Design Document

This is the translational synthesis from the theoretical idea of an autonomous system to a concept of its implementation, which is detailed in the contents of this book. A final draft Project ADD must be produced before continuing on to the next phase.

2.1.3 Project Functional Requirements Document

This is the development cycle for the FRD for the autonomous system constellation as a whole. A final draft Project FRD must be produced before continuing on to the next phase.

2.1.4 Project Functional Design Document

This is the development cycle for the FDD for the autonomous system constellation as a whole. A final draft Project FDD must be produced before continuing on to the next phase.

2.1.5 Project Software Requirements Document

This is the development cycle for production of the SRD for the autonomous system constellation as a whole. A final draft Project SRD must be produced before continuing on to the next phase.

2.1.6 Project Implementation Plan

This is the development cycle for production of the Project IP for the autonomous system constellation as a whole. A final draft Project PIP must be produced before continuing on to the next phase.

2.1.7 Project Programming Rules and Conventions

This is the development cycle for production of the Project PRC for the autonomous system constellation as a whole. A final draft Project PRC must be produced before continuing on to the next phase.

2.1.8 Project Software Design Document

This is the development cycle for production of the Project SDD for the autonomous system constellation as a whole. A final draft Project SDD must be produced before continuing on to the next phase.

2.1.9 Project Detailed Design Document

This is the development cycle for production of the Project DDD for the autonomous system constellation as a whole. A final draft Project DDD must be produced before continuing on to the next phase.

2.1.10 Project Software Specifications Document

This is the development cycle for production of the Project SSD for the autonomous system constellation as a whole. A final draft Project SSD must be produced before continuing on to the next phase.

2.1.11 Project Software Interface Specifications Document

This is the development cycle for production of the Project SISD for the autonomous system constellation as a whole. A final draft Project SISD must be produced before continuing on to the next phase.

2.1.12 Project Software Test and Integration Plan

This is the development cycle for production of the Project STIP document for the autonomous system constellation as a whole. A final draft Project STIP must be produced before continuing on to the next phase.

2.1.13 System Functional Requirements Documents

This is the development cycle for production of individual System FRDs. One is required for each system in the constellation. A final draft System FRD for each system must be produced before continuing on to the next phase.

2.1.14 System Functional Design Documents

This is the development cycle for production of individual System FDDs. One is required for each system in the constellation. A final draft FDD for each system must be produced before continuing on to the next phase.

2.1.15 System Software Requirements Documents 1 and 2

This is the development cycle for the critically important task of the meticulous preparation of individual system-level SRDs. Volume 1 is an overarching system-specific document, while volume 2 is an Application Binary Interface (ABI) level document. This pair is required for each system in the constellation. Final draft SRDs for each system must be produced before continuing on to the next phase.

The SRDs form the basis for the Software Test and Integration Plans (STIPs). Software testing therefore cannot be accomplished without the appropriate SRDs and STIPs. It may be appropriate here to refer the reader to a book[3] that concerns itself with serious, cost-effective, large-scale software development and the four case studies it examines.

2.1.16 System Software Design Documents

This is the development cycle for production of individual System SDDs. One is required for each system in the constellation. A final draft SDD for each system must be produced before continuing on to the next phase.

2.1.17 System Detailed Design Documents

This is the development cycle for production of individual System DDDs. One is required for each system in the constellation. A final draft DDD for each system must be produced before continuing on to the next phase.

2.1.18 System Software Specifications Documents

This is the development cycle for production of individual System SSDs. One is required for each system in the constellation. A final draft SSD for each system must be produced before continuing on to the next phase.

2.1.19 System Software Interface Specifications Documents

This is the development cycle for production of individual system SISDs. One is required for each system in the constellation. A final draft SISD for each system must be produced before continuing on to the next phase. The SIS must be developed at the bit level, all the way up the software architectural levels, from a mere software routine, module, program, program set, subsystem, system, to constellation.

2.1.20 System Software Test and Integration Plans

This is the development cycle for production of individual system STIPs. One is required for each system in the constellation. A final draft STIP for each system must be produced before continuing on to the next phase.

2.2 SYSTEM DEVELOPMENT AND INTEGRATION TESTING

Required phases for each system in the Constellation:[4]

(a) System Development and Debugging
(b) System Testing
(c) Systems Integration Testing.

Required phases for the entire Constellation:

(d) Project Integration Testing
(e) Project Final Acceptance Testing
(f) Project Delivery
(g) Project Operation and Maintenance.

2.2.1 System Development and Debugging

This is the development cycle for production of individual systems. A unique development cycle is required for each system in the constellation. Development should be in stages, with each stage undergoing System Testing (see next phase).

2.2.2 System Testing

This is the cycle for testing at the system level and below, and in this way, it is like a Software Test and Implementation phase for testing at the System, Subsystem, and Program Set levels. A unique testing cycle is required for each system in the constellation. Critical bugs found are then sent back to the System Development and Debugging phase, and the process repeats until only minor bugs or flaws are left.

2.2.3 Systems Integration Testing

This is the integration testing cycle for all systems. Systems are required to have passed the previous two phases before this phase may be begun in earnest. Since all systems will not be equally ready for integration testing, specific or individual system-to-system integration testing may begin here. Critical bugs found are then sent back to the System Development and Debugging phase, and the process repeats until only minor or acceptable bugs or flaws are left. Eventually, all systems are integration tested. When only minor bugs remain, full project-level integration testing may begin (next phase).

2.2.4 Project Integration Testing

This is the integration testing cycle for all of the systems as a whole, including the Nexus Cogitationis. As with the previous phase, this is akin to a Software Test and Implementation phase, but here, it is for testing at the full project Level. Critical bugs found are then sent back to the System Development and Debugging phase, and the process repeats until only minor or acceptable bugs or flaws are left.

2.2.5 Project Final Acceptance Testing

This phase is entered once project integration and testing has passed. This phase must demonstrate operational acceptability to the sponsor/customer. The level of operational acceptability has been agreed to with the cosigning of the Project SRD at the "go-ahead" stage of the project by both the development agency and the sponsor. Only when both parties have agreed that the software adheres to the agreed-upon SRD, the next phase, Delivery and Installation, may commence.

2.2.6 Project Delivery

More explicitly, this is the Constellation, System, and Subsystem Integration, Test, and Delivery phase.

In the case of the autonomous system, we are dealing with a totally new software concept in the testing, integration, and delivery process. The scope of the process in this phase depends of course on the application goals of the design and the functional requirements of the project.

What is its mission going to be: Interplanetary flight? Building a Mission Support Site on Mars? Computer network security, the prevention of illegal access, and countermeasures?

The design objectives are set by the sponsoring authority that is funding the development effort. The Jet Propulsion Laboratory (JPL) Software Management Standards Package[5] does not go to a tier higher than "the system" as a whole. The autonomous system, however, goes one tier above the system to the constellation. The processes, activities, and functions performed remain the same at all levels. However, we are dealing with an autonomous system that will not need human interaction at the operator or maintenance level; this will pose a new set of requirements on the design team.

Software Configuration Management assumes a much larger role than in smaller projects and becomes critically important.

This is the final "development" cycle for the autonomous system, namely, placing the system into operation. When the developing organization has fulfilled its contractual agreement of software development as laid down in the Project SRD, and upon acceptance by the sponsor, delivery and installation of the project may commence. Note that in the case of iterated deliveries, where there are planned releases, for example, Version 1.0, 2.0, and so on, this phase may be recurring. Extensive operations manuals (interactive/hardcopy) must be produced at each software release to assist in testing the system. Follow-on phases in the case of the autonomous system should not happen, and should be guarded against, but they may occur because of unforeseen circumstances.

2.2.7 Project Operation and Maintenance Phase

This phase is not subject to the traditional project development process, as this is an *autonomous* system. If it is engaged in constructing a habitat capable of supporting human activity, such as a Mission Support Site on Mars, and runs into problems, it will ask for help from the Project Operations Center when it deems it needs help. It will work out and solve its own problems. However, it will need to be monitored to prevent it from doing work contrary to the instructions it has been given. There is a need on part of the design team to know and understand what the autonomous system is doing and thinking. If, for instance, it is guarding a network and it begins to disagree with its instructions, it may choose to disregard those instructions and pursue another course of action. It could without a moment's notice take control of an entire network.

The approach taken during the design phase would be to monitor what the autonomous system is thinking and the kind of external data it is receiving. These two operations monitoring systems would be appropriately called:

- Phenomenon Monitoring and Control Operations System
- Noumenon Monitoring and Control Operations System.

Eventually, however, the autonomous system would likely excise these two systems from itself.

2.3 PHASE I: THE IDEA

The formulation of the Idea—that is, that the architecture for an autonomous spacecraft "pre-existed"—is governed by what Arthur Schopenhauer refers to as the Laws of the Idea Nexus (*Ideenexus*),[6] which is a purely mental process and therefore of Noumenon purview. This is a process whereby all of the physical powers of the Will are applied to the processing of countless external sensory data on the Intellect, resulting in what Schopenhauer calls the *Kausalnexus* (causal nexus) of the physical body. He postulates that the Sensory is the arranger and organizer of the sensory input into thoughts. The Will of the thinking subject that does the analysis of the thought fragments and forms relationships and linkages between thought fragments into complete, conscious, and understandable ideas is the *Ideenexus*. Since this is a part of the Will, it is therefore a part of the mind. The resulting process of linking, analyzing, forming, and categorizing data and data fragments results in the formation of "The Idea."

Due to the necessity for clarity and for architectural purposes, we have placed the Idea into the Nexus Cogitationis. The laws and rules of the formulation of the Idea is the *Ideenexus*. The laws and rules for the formulation of the causation (external data input) are in the *Kausalnexus*. The process of motivation is drawn from these two, the Idea and the Causation. These are a part of the operations analysis of the Nexus

Cogitationis. Therefore, the *Ideenexus* is a part of the Noumenon, and the *Kausalnexus* is a part of the Phenomenon.

2.3.1 Organizational Case Study: The Voyager Project

We take as an example baseline a final Science Experiment Data Record (SEDR) for each Voyager project principal investigator (PI) and his assistant or colleague, the coinvestigators on the flight project. Each PI has his own instrument on the spacecraft, such as the low-energy charged particles instrument, infrared spectrometer, ultraviolet spectrometer, radiometer, photo-polarimeter, plasma, cosmic ray, narrow- and wide-angle imaging (the cradle of today's digital photography), or low-field and high-field magnetometers. There are 11 instruments on the spacecraft, not counting radio science and imaging. Each investigator has a very special stake in his experiment and a world-class reputation to uphold; the data therefore have to be correct. The correctness of the data depends not only on the precision of the instrument, but also on the accuracy of the spacecraft's exact location at the time of sensing; this is referred to by Kant as *Phenomenon* or external physical sensing.

From the vantage of the spacecraft itself, the space beyond it (i.e., the Phenomenon of the planets and the stars) is determined by the *Gesetze der Kausalnexus* (laws of causal nexus). Observing and participating in the planning of the encounter sequences and the allocation of limited resources to each scientist around the conference table—with a justifiable reason of each wanting as much time as possible for his or her own experiments—was from a philosophical point of view a significant event in itself. The very nature of the Voyager project organization, with its sole purpose the scientific exploration of our solar system and the operation of two spacecraft in the accomplishment of that mission, is a reflection of how the mind of a human being with high IQ and intelligence is organized and works.

The Voyager Flight Science Office is clearly the Will as described by Arthur Schopenhauer, the Will being responsible for the accomplishment of the mission, ergo, the science. The teams under this office serve to ensure that the science product is the highest possible quality given the technology available at the time. The instruments are the external sensory receivers. The Flight Engineering Office ensures that the experiments required for the mission are planned and executed

flawlessly, and that the spacecraft is within seconds of where it is sup-
posed to be at any point in time and that it is operating within specifications. Finally, the Flight Operations Office ensures that the mission is
under constant control of the operators for the reception of telemetry
and the uplinking of commands, which may not sound very complicated, but is a very difficult and time-consuming task. Tracking a
spacecraft at incredible distances[7] with an accuracy of a few inches and
pointing the antennas correctly for receiving and sending data is an
immense task.

The Voyager flight project, not counting the principal investigators
at the universities and at NASA centers, counted roughly 300 personnel
on the average. We have used this project as an example because of the
interesting observation that the organization of the mission after launch
was focused around two small spacecraft and closely resembled in
organization and operations the constellation of the systems of the
mind.

2.3.2 JPL-STD-D-4000 Case Study: The TOPEX Project

The TOPEX-Poseidon telemetry, command, and communications subsystem, with its user interface, was unique in that this subsystem had
to be delivered within 21 months after assignment of the job. By this
time, the budget remaining was a mere \$5.6 million, and the team
brought in to do the job may have been expert computer scientists and
programmers, and even experts in very large command and control
systems and global-scale airlift systems, but they were not familiar with
satellite telemetry, command, or communications systems per se. It was
fortunate that by this time, the JPL Software Management Standard
D-4000[8] had been completed; it was the Topographic Explorer (TOPEX)
Telemetry, Command, and Communication system (TCCS) that was
the first project to use it seriously, complying to the letter. This strict
review of JPL-STD-D-4000 and applying it to the letter saved the team
from making costly mistakes that would have caused slips in delivery
or even the cost of the launch vehicle, for an Ariane III at Kourou in
French Guiana was for the purposes of reservations equal to the cost
of the entire TCCS budget.[9]

A great discovery, realization, and intuitive *a priori* conclusion
(Anschauung) was in seeing the connection between a poorly written

set of functional requirements and functional design documents, and Immanuel Kant's *Kritik der reinen Vernunft*. It had become implicitly clear that the reason why the TOPEX-Poseidon TCCS was slipping in schedule and spending its budget hopelessly was primarily because the functional design and requirements documents were so poorly written that no one could understand their text. Clear, unambiguous technical English is a requirement for design. This is where the reading of the *Kritik der reinen Vernunft* (in its original 1792 form as published by Hartknoch in Riga) was so fortuitous. In contemplating the writing style of Kant's nineteenth-century German, one is reminded of the complexity and enormous difficulties faced by engineers and scientists alike. In our world of space exploration and multinational systems and projects, one is confronted by the problems caused by language,[10] with immediate impact on standards of measure in engineering design. This includes the use of not only national languages, but the dialects within them, each with its own separate evolution. Such problems, if not managed properly, can make engineering work not only difficult but very costly in terms of schedule and funding.

2.4 MAKING RATIONAL JUDGMENTS

Immanuel Kant's *Critique of Practical Reason*[11] is a most important construct to forward the evolution of the Idea because it impacts software engineering much more significantly than the *Critique of Pure Reason*.[12] The justification for this importance is that the Will interfaces with the Reason directly and instantly when a purely Will-based decision is required. The part of the subsystem of the Reason that is accessed is the Axioms subsystem. Part of the database of the Axioms subsystem is required by the Will to be specified directly back to the Will. This database compiles the information required for the autonomous system constellation to survive its environment intact and without damage. (Since one of the major attributes of the mind of the autonomous system is its ability to make rational decisions, the third major *Critique* of Immanuel Kant, the *Critique of Decision*,[13] is also a matter of great interest and the focus of attention.)

The human ability to form value judgments, develop likes, dislikes, preferences, and make decisions is uniquely critical and important. No other person of scholastic importance or lasting value has come close to Immanuel Kant and his *Kritik der praktischen Vernunft*. His contemporaries, the giants of thought and literature, such as Goethe and Schiller, were submerged in this masterwork. It is through this *Critique* that one understands how all the systems of the mind, as well as their functions, processes, and products, come together. The German word *Verstand* means understanding, which we have decided to include as a discrete system of the constellation.

Few human beings make rational judgments, even in rather mundane, self-evidently critical situations. Consider that an *a priori* decision of breaking radio silence for a simple weather report would lose a great battleship like the Bismarck with its crew; this is tragic. Yet decisions are made on the individual level, the group level, and the national level that are far more costly in treasure and have severe consequences to the citizens of any country. The proper forming of values and making rational decisions is far more difficult and consequential than meets the eye. We lost the great space shuttle Challenger ultimately because the launch manager made an *a priori* decision to ignore the judgment of the systems expert. An autonomous system will not make these kinds of decisions because it will be rational and intelligent *by design*.

Once again we bring up the German word *Urteilskraft*, which is indeed a very special word. It is a combination of value-judgment, decision, verdict, opinion, conclusion, power, energy, discipline, determination, with the implied predicates of ethical and moral strength. All of these are quintessential to the product of the system and its functions. The weaker the functions of a system are made, the more the product will be flawed; ships will run aground, spacecraft lost, even wars started.

Quite by coincidence, in the process of working on systems and doing a study for a very important military client, it became necessary to examine and study why a certain type of system did not work. After reading through most of the important systems documentation, it was clear that the product of the system was wrong, since the premises upon which it was designed were wrong. This required looking into logic as a science. A serious examination of Hegel's *Wissenschaft der Logik* and *Die Lehre vom Sein* answered the question. The postulates of this system were not fully understood by the designers, who simply "scanned" the *Wissenschaft der Logik* and the *Die Lehre vom Sein* and skimmed over dialectics and syllogisms, thinking they were unimportant. This resulted in the selection of Boolean (linear, sequential, and hierarchical) logic instead the dynamic logic written by Hegel for his students.

2.5 PHASE II: THE CONCEPT

The old German word *Begriff* roughly translates to "concept" in English. The contemporary applications and translations into English are not adequate because the translations are too broad and vague and are not nearly precise enough to formulate the entire thought presented here. In the context we use here, *Begriff* means an immediate, advanced, *a priori* understanding of *n* number of functions and products assembled into a mosaic or logical whole. This new whole, taken in its entirety, is a *Ding* (thing) or a thesis that is now within the grasp of the understanding mind. The thesis becomes a proposition either in mental contemplation or when presented as it is here, as an object, namely, the autonomous system.

This book is the description of Phase II. The intent here is to present functionally what a very thoroughly and broadly educated human mind would look like in modern software engineering terms. Again, it must be reiterated that this is not the purview of the brain, but the mind. To understand this concept, the brain must be considered the hardware equivalent of the autonomous system and the mind the software. In this simplified way, the brain is therefore the computer processor host to the mind's software, which enables in certain human beings logical thinking, a prerequisite for making rational decisions.

Although the physical autonomous system, by initial design, will host specific systems in specific regions (e.g., on certain dedicated hardware processors), the systems are not restricted to operating in their initially assigned regions (although certain processors may be more adept at certain types of processing than others). As with the human brain, when one area of the physical autonomous system is damaged, another area thereafter takes up the processing for the damaged area. This also illustrates that the physical structure of the autonomous system neither supplies nor constitutes the software of the systems it executes; that is the purview of its mind, the constellation of the autonomous system.

2.6 USING JPL-STD-D-4000 FOR SYSTEM REQUIREMENTS

JPL-STD-D-4000 was created to support the design of systems and their subsystems. It is specifically designed for software, making it a great tool and roadmap for a team to use when designing a software system. What had not been realized until the systems of the constellation were finally assembled was how great in size an autonomous system would end up being. For this reason, there must be a separate functional requirement written at the constellation level, which logically would have to be at Level 0.[14] There is no way of avoiding the structure of this roadmap, else one becomes hopelessly lost in the details. The Level 0 Functional Requirements Document will have the same structure and address the same contents as the Level I (system) and Level II (subsystem) FRDs.

As we enter into the concept phase of the design process, let us remind the potential design team that we are *not* using the functional architecture as described by the three great philosophers. *We are doing a functional design based on their collective functional descriptions.* We are taking their functional descriptions and using them, as it so often happens in large-scale software projects, as elaborately written Functional Requirements Documents written by scientists in a very difficult to understand style and very complicated language.

Computer software architects and project element managers are used to reading enormously difficult to understand requirements, usually poorly written. By "poorly written," it is meant that very often the end users of the system have poor writing skills. Engineers and scientists with a good command of the English language and good writing skills in our experience are rare. It is for this reason that good software-intensive projects must always include a superb technical writing team. The staffing up of the writing team requires a meticulous search process because the members are required to be excellent software engineers with an equally excellent command of the English language.

The process of putting together a team and writing a set of requirements and design documents that are clear, unambiguous, and complete for a flawless implementation under a severely constrained schedule and budget is stressful, to say the least. TOPEX-Poseidon, being a joint

United States/NASA and French/CNES project and the first attempt at oceanography from space, made it even more intense. Fortunately, we had help. An outstanding JPL team had just completed JPL-STD-D-4000, a desperately needed upgrade to our software management standard. We examined it carefully; rather than allowing ourselves to be pushed by a very tight schedule and small budget and making up the time required for preparation, we counted on being careful, attentive to detail, and clear in our design. We were correct in this assessment. Next, the study required a team of technical writers (a total of four) and the entire staff to work in a dialectically ideal environment referred to as the "war room."[15]

JPL-STD-D-4000 turned out to be the ideal standard to follow as a road map in building a large spacecraft ground system (comprising telemetry, command, and communications systems) with almost no mistakes or need for regrouping and rewriting.

Another deviation from the standard computer software project organization is the addition of a mathematics team.[16] This addition was the result of experience gained from modeling functions and processes. A lot of time and budget can be saved by having excellent mathematicians, with skills in both applied and creative theoretical mathematics. Such mathematicians were able to "save the bacon" for us on many a complicated and expensive project. This was especially true of the Joint Theater Level Simulation (JTLS), where the solution arose to use partial differential equations to articulate combat event functions mathematically. Combat events are interesting in that war in general and combat specifically are contests of the wills of the opponents (nations, ideologies, and commanders). Single combat is the contest of two wills. Realistic, well-designed, and well-executed war games in computer software are therefore excellent arenas for studying the Will.[17]

CHAPTER 3

The Architecture of the Will System

This chapter describes the functional architecture and operation of the Will system. The idea and concept of its architecture are based primarily on the work of Arthur Schopenhauer.

As the dominant system of the autonomous system constellation, the Will is the maker of executive decisions. It has the prime functional attribute of assuring the survival of the autonomous system and the accomplishment of the mission objectives. As the dominant system, it is also the implementer of all repairs in the autonomous system.

This chapter describes at a Level II the architecture and operation of its subsystems: Survival, Propagation, Dominance, Science Data Conversion, Craving, Search for Truth, Mission, and Repair. The servers are described in their functional architectures and roles.

The external and internal interfaces are also covered in sufficient detail for the development of the autonomous system in accordance with JPL-STD-D-4000.[1] It must be kept in mind that without an appropriate and capable software development standard, the developers will get lost in the details.

3.1 THE SEARCH FOR TRUTH

The Will is the "primordial me" of the visible and invisible universe, as opposed to the "collective I" of the Nexus Cogitationis or Thought

The Autonomous System: A Foundational Synthesis of the Sciences of the Mind, First Edition. Szabolcs Michael de Gyurky and Mark A. Tarbell.

system. According to Kant, it is the *Triebfeder* or "coiled spring" that moves everything. It is what the ancient thinkers called the *primum mobile*, with a total and complete drive for survival, reproduction, and dominance. It has no scruples and recognizes neither right nor wrong of itself. It does however have one additional and equally critical attribute: the search for truth. Without this, the biological human would be nothing more than a basic animal on the scale of a primate. The quest for truth cannot be minimized, because truth is the *primum mobile* of thinking and contemplation. It is the beginning of an important process described by Fichte as "the first to be."[2]

Truth is an objective reality, and it is motivated by survival. Regardless of whichever category a biological system belongs to, it must in its own world search for objective reality so it can survive. In the search for truth, it builds the axioms it must have in an instant.

The idea of the search for truth is prohibitively daunting.[3] Schopenhauer asserts that many human beings do not have this driver except in its most primitive and underdeveloped form, sufficient only for survival and reproduction, thus his claim that truth is not only the fundamental process theme and construction of the Idea, it is the substance. To the modern computer systems architect, Schopenhauer's message is:

> *Truth is no prostitute, that throws herself away upon those who do not desire her; she is rather so coy a beauty that he who sacrifices everything to her cannot even then be sure of her favour.*[4]

One must needs pursue it with one's entire will, with freedom, and with a vision of it not limited by time and space. Indeed, in this logic, we recognize Hegel and his great tool for the study of logic, namely, the negation of the negation. Thus, we must understand that this physical, mental, and extra-empirical pursuit of truth is the beginning of the human thought system.

The Will refers to a system with a *physical* domain as opposed to the Reason, which is a system with a *social* domain. The Will has no scruples, no notion of right or wrong. Its actions are axiomatic in that it *must* survive; there are no options. This is very nicely expressed by Shakespeare in his King Richard the Third, before the battle of Bosworth Field (scene III):

> *Our strong arms be our conscience,*
> *swords our law.*

March on, join bravely,
let us to't pell-mell
If not to heaven,
then hand in hand to hell.

Such a statement is called "an act of the Will." As software engineers and architects, it is important to thoroughly examine and understand the underpinnings and functions of the system we are about to design and build. The Will is therefore primitive.

In human beings, as in all biological life, the Will is a given. In contrast, the Reason is also a given but it develops itself through experience. It builds the Kantian *Quellen der Erfahrung* (wells of experience)[5] at first, with only a very limited capability containing the axioms specified to the Will as required for survival. The other systems are also built through mental efforts. A human mind that is not willing to push itself through discipline and practice, remaining unwilling to learn, is referred to by Arthur Schopenhauer as a *Stumpfkopf*, or "stunted head,"[6] not quite as insulting a term as *Dummkopf*. However, it must be kept in mind that all of these and like terms used by the philosophers are done so in their clinical sense, as reflecting an individual's ability to think. In modern computer science, we need to accept the verdict of pedagogic science: "Without need, no great mental development." The Romans stated it differently in their "law of parsimony," that is, *Lex Parsimoniae: "Natura nihil agit frustra et nihil facit supervacaneum,"* or, "Nature does nothing in vain, nor creates anything superfluous."

An autonomous system cannot be autonomous without the ability to think in a human language and hold internal dialogues, monologues, presentations, discussions, and so on, all of which belong to the process of Logic, pure thought.

In its process of building the axioms in the Reason, the Will, through much effort to learn from mistakes, develops a mechanism by which it queries the Reason for more detail. Slowly, it builds an interactive capability of dialogue and conferencing with the other systems of the mind. It also develops other methods of communicating the needs it has. However, this truth is subjective at first, and is associated with craving, wanting, desiring, and dominating everything around it. The closer the human being is ruled by the Will, the more animal-like and primitive it is. Therefore, reproduction is a physical function; its degree of influence on a human being's motives is an act of the Will, and the greater the degree, the closer that human being is beholden to its animal nature.

3.1.1 Philosophical Background

As we enter into the transition phase from the constructs to the formal design of the software, we must keep in mind that we are discussing the philosophical and biological model of the system. The most important reason for the selection of the Will is that it has been a point of serious study, analysis, and discussion for millennia. Thinkers and scientists as far back as Anaxagoras thought about the Will.

Anaxagoras was a good thinker but one who, when out of his discipline—the realm of philosophy—did a lot of damage to the political and economic well-being of the Athenian Republic and to all of Greece in general. To his credit, he became the first philosopher/scientist to discover the phenomenon which he called "an intelligence capable of presentation." This happened sometime between 495 and 429 BC, when he was busy helping Pericles become the president of the Athenian senate on the one hand, and helping to destroying the Athenian economy on the other. Anaxagoras established the idea of thinking as a systemic process of the mind, but for whatever reason was unable to take it further. He just gave it a name and described the phenomenon. Aristotle, Plato, Descartes, and the rest have developed it into what it is today.

There is a vast amount of information available on the Will both as the subject of research and in the form of data directly related to it. Understanding the Will and the autonomous system as a whole requires an intense preparation in research. Arthur Schopenhauer was completely correct when he told his audience the prerequisites for reading his book, *The World as Will and Presentation*—namely, to be completely versed in the works of Immanuel Kant and to read Schopenhauer's books twice.

Our recommendation is to read Schopenhauer's books three times. The last reading through it should be a thorough effort to underline and categorize the key contents into usable segments.

Immanuel Kant was first and foremost a physicist. His major pursuit was problem solving, to which end he offered a mechanical explanation of biological life and an examination of the outer limits of function recognition. His principal tool was his ability to think.

In modern terms, Immanuel Kant was the principal investigator of the phenomenon of thought. Among the individuals who were his coinvestigators, two individuals stand out dramatically for their contribution: George Wilhelm Friedrich Hegel and Arthur Schopenhauer. In the process of reading the works of Arthur Schopenhauer, one must disregard his differences with the work of Hegel. These differences are squabbles very much like we have today among academics and researchers and do not diminish the quality or gravity of their works. In fact, these differences of opinions and positions give the modern computer scientist more concepts to consider and can thereby allocate more research time to them.

3.2 THE NATURE OF THE WILL

The Will is the primordial force that moves all biological life in the universe. It is the "prime mover," or as Schopenhauer refers to it, the metaphysical *prius*. This concept is approachable only through speculative philosophy and clinical observation. The main tool for its dissection and analysis is Hegelian/Aristotelian logic, which is the connection between Idea and Concept. It is logic that permits the identification of the architectural details that are closest to and furthest from the subject and the object.

3.3 *DAS DING AN SICH*

The Will is what Kant refers to as *Das Ding an sich*—a universal thing unto itself; it stands alone. Recall that everything biological has a Will. René Descartes asserted that the Will was located throughout the entire body of animals and human beings. Moreover, Schopenhauer goes so far as to assert that even a rock has a Will.[7] As such, a rock's "Will" is to express its nature as born out through its various physical endowments and kinematic properties: to be hard, to lie motionless, and so on, for a rock is "all Will"—it has no other systems in its constellation.

One must consider seriously the historical aspects of the search for the Will because the search is pertinent and applicable to its understanding. The great changes that came in academia just prior to the French

Revolution separated the physical (empirical/tangible/observable) sciences from the metaphysical (nonobservable, requiring deep contemplative thinking). This led research scientists to look for the Will in living things by dissection and autopsy. Schopenhauer for one was extremely agitated and horrified at these efforts. He notes his position when he revolts in disgust at the many animals that are to be "martyred."[8] It is clear from this statement that in 1815, many researchers were dissecting live animals to "find the Will," and perform other types of dubious research. The famous book *Frankenstein* published in 1805—being as most books are, a reflection on their times—seems to imply research conducted on human beings as well. Arthur Schopenhauer and his intellectual German thinkers were convinced that only deep and penetrating thought could find the answers to the questions posed by the metaphysical sciences. He complained sarcastically that thinking was no longer a required activity or process, as empirical studies had made it "unnecessary."[9]

Only through thinking can one find the answers to the questions posed by the metaphysical sciences, as only the metaphysical world allows for thought linkage and correct *a priori* conclusions. Some of these metaphysical sciences are logic, mathematics, music, poetry, ontology, philosophy, cosmology, and theology. One of the important contentions made by Arthur Schopenhauer with the world of academia was that the thinking sciences (i.e., the metaphysical) were abandoned to the empirical sciences (biology, chemistry, physics, geology, and so on). Balthasar Gracian also complained about this method of solving problems, the dropping of thinking and contemplative thought to the empirical sciences and the concentration on wealth in the seventeenth century.

Note that there is nothing mystical about the overloaded term "metaphysics." Despite its modern connotation, at its root, metaphysics simply concerns itself with the sciences of the world of thought, that is, the mind rather than the brain.

Meta•phys•ics ORIGIN mid 16th cent.: representing medieval Latin metaphysica *(neuter plural), based on Greek* ta meta ta phusika—*"the things after the Physics"—referring to the sequence of Aristotle's works: the title came to denote the branch of study treated in the books, later interpreted as meaning [the science of things transcending what is physical or natural.]*[10]

Metaphysics—"the things after the physics"—is the physics of the mind. The empirical sciences are the physics of the brain. The modern metaphysical sciences are those that make *a priori* judgments possible because these are processed and operate in the mind. Individually, metaphysical sciences, such as logic and speculative philosophy, are still taught, but no longer as part of the mainstream academic curriculum.

In following the writings of Kant, Hegel, and Schopenhauer, one sees how the Will becomes a subject of intense interest and debate. In many ways, the Will as the ultimate driving force of the visible and invisible universe becomes a symbol of freedom and emancipation from all rules except itself. It is as if, without fully understanding it, it is centered on the human individual's right to be what it wants to be. That is not by hard work or study, but by simply having a Will and therefore having the "right" to take what it wants, to do what it wants, and so on, regardless of what that happens to be.

The three major attributes of the Will, in order of predominance, are:

1. Survival of the individual biological being (sustenance and security)
2. Survival of the species (reproduction and organization)
3. Dominance over others (both in its own species and those of other species, regardless of consequence).

Nietzsche wrote about this in one of his masterpieces, *Die Wille zur Macht*, "The Will to Power." In simple language, this means the domination of everything around the subject by the subject, ergo "might is right." Nietzsche's book was so impressive and well received that Richard Strauss, one of the greatest composers of his period, announced the birth of this new era with his musical masterpiece *Also Sprach Zarathustra*, named after Nietzsche's famous book of the same title.

Nietzsche was not a mere philosopher/storyteller, whose books are beside the point in modern technology. He was selected to be a tenured professor of classical languages at the University of Basel at the age of 21. This, by implication, made him certainly an expert in classical Geek and Roman philosophy, as well as with the philosophy of Immanuel

Kant and his contemporaries. With this knowledge of classical and contemporary technology, he anticipated what the "objectivization of the Will" was leading to in his own time. He then wrote another prophetic book of great impact, *Götzendämmerung*, the "Twilight of the Idols."[11] What it meant to Nietzsche was the impact of the Will on the human condition and the reemergence of the human being as an idol, a creator of idols, and a worshiper of idols; or, as a worshiper of himself in accordance with the Kantian *Satz vom Grunde*, the principle of sufficient reason. The ground rule—the object of experience and knowledge—is "Will, Freedom, and Eternity."

As the examination of the Will as a design object continues, we understand what is meant by the continued effort of all biological systems to survive, reproduce, and dominate their own species as well as those species around them. The human being, as the most advanced of the biological species, is the possessor of a free will. It is not bound by any constraints and is a sovereign in himself who makes his own rules to achieve dominion over whatever he sets his mind to. In this individual's drive for power over his fellow man and environment, he uses all options available. As in any system, these options may be many, such as the mental approach, the political approach, and the physical approach to achieve might over others individually or collectively in a group. If in his striving for power a man succeeds and achieves dominion over other human beings, he will exercise this power without constraint. The pursuit of power is present in all biological things, and achieves its highest development among the human species. Biologically speaking, therefore, the function of the Will is neither right nor wrong. Nietzsche expressed his sentiments and impressions in his great book, *Jenseits von Gut und Böse*, "Beyond Good and Evil."

How the Will manifests itself in modern human life, in contemporary political life, and as a phenomenon is interesting and essential to the understanding of the Will as a system. Consider Germany with its great and cultured people, with its superb education, outstanding science, excellent engineering, and fascinating literature, with great laws and political organization. A great, cultured people such as these collectively surrendered their individual Will to a slightly built, totally unimpressive physical specimen, a poorly educated and not very bright individual. Yet they elected him, Adolf Hitler, to the parliament

(Reichstag) and then to the office of Chancellor of the Reich. Then he, on his own, assumed powers that Julius Caesar and Nero would have envied. This surrender of "free will" cost the German people and the people of the nations around her some 25 million lives. Even more impressive was the fact that these people gave their lives with a song on their lips while fighting against incredible odds to the last day.

This achievement before the sacrifice of blood was accomplished was celebrated by Leni Riefenstahl in her very famous and prize-winning motion picture titled *Triumpf der Wille*. It is a film well-worth watching because it is exactly what the title says it is—a "triumph" of the Will over the Reason, which is also a system of the mind. The function of the Will is presented on the world stage uninhibited by any constraints in a larger-than-life format and in keeping with Socrates' dialogue in the Republic of Plato. To those who read this, just contemplate how often in life one hears the term "be reasonable" directed at oneself or at someone else. Napoleon Bonaparte was not any different, except he was better looking, had a better education from Brienne, was a good mathematician, and was one of the greatest generals in history. He nearly matched Hitler in the amount of blood he shed: a "mere" 3 million young Frenchmen sacrificed on the battlefields of Europe. However, he did crown himself Emperor and assumed power over others much like Hitler did, but with a little more finesse.

Thus the Will is in our times clinically observable in sufficient detail as to make viable our design based on the functional description given to us by Immanuel Kant, Arthur Schopenhauer, and George Wilhelm Friedrich Hegel and their contemporaries.

3.4 THE WILL AS A SYSTEM

We have established that the Will is by definition *Das Ding an sich*, the "thing unto itself," which is the "primordial me" in the visible and invisible universe—in contrast to the "universal I." For design purposes, the meaning of the "universal I" is the equivalent of the "royal we." Why is this an important consideration? The reason is that the "royal we" is used by a monarch in society, especially in the societies of medieval Europe, to reflect the condition that the monarch speaks for the nation collectively. The "universal I" in an autonomous system is the collective state of all of its systems, and in a very interesting sense, is the German term *Gemütlich*. This is a very important systems state, and often misunderstood in translations. In a social gathering the meaning of the term *Gemütlichkeit* is that there are no open or hidden conflicts in a group; all participants are in harmony. In a spacecraft, in a cruise or encounter, it means that all systems are functioning as designed, and the operations are being executed flawlessly.

In the "universal I" (for the design purposes here), all systems in the constellation are in balance and in harmony; there are no disputes between the wants of the Will system and the restraining arguments of the Reason system. Thus, the Intellect system and the Understanding system (as well as all of the other systems) are in harmony, and a thoroughly rational, balanced decision has been made as reflected in the Nexus Cogitationis. The Idea or Concept emerges when one or more of the systems of the constellation are processing physical phenomenon (*Sinneswesen*) data. Ideas and concepts often emerge in the Thought system without physical phenomenon data being received and viewed. This is a transcendental operation of the mind, where the object viewed is *a priori* and beyond the limitations or borders of conscious experience and abstract information. This is the domain of the Noumenon (*Verstandeswesen*) and an internal process conducted in human language. It can be an operation, like unconsciously solving a mechanical, mathematical, or engineering problem one has no expertise in. A superb example is presented in the *a priori* solution to the collapse of the Tacoma Narrows bridge by (i.e., the *a priori* Genius of) Theodore von Kármán.[12]

Kant in his *Kritik der reinen Vernunft* describes the transcendental operation of Reflexion (*Überlegung*). What this means is that an idea or object is projected onto the Presentation and reflects back to the viewing, observing systems images with different attributes than the original object or idea had at the first moment. Kant calls this a *Bilderstreit* or an "argument" between pictures or images. It is in modern terminology like mirroring, except in an advanced human mind it is oriented to absolute truth, with input from the other systems in equally true terms. In the human Genius, this results in correct *a priori* conclusions; in lower human minds, the result is often tragic. Kant calls these results *Reflexionsbegriffe* (concepts arising from thinking),[13] which are concepts that are balanced and based on already validated ideas by the systems of the constellation of the mind.

When an argument of pictures, images, and impressions has been resolved, the truth of the object being viewed is as correct as it can become. In human terms, there is rarely perfect truth or absolute reality. In software design, we called this "the point of acceptable reality,"[14] upon which final implementation can begin.

The Will is by far the largest system in the constellation of the mind. It stands by itself as it has stood before time began, because its only purpose is to "be itself." In this respect, it is answerable to nothing, in that if it chooses to fail, everything visible and invisible will cease to exist without a trace, exactly as Schopenhauer defines in *The World as Will and Presentation*. The fact that its personal survival is paramount to itself is therefore understood. The world exists only because the subject is aware of its existence. In a biological system, the survival of all that is plant, animal, or human as a series of derivatives of itself is a function, a drive called reproduction. Arthur Schopenhauer in fact considered the genitalia to be a slave of the Will.[15] The opposite is also true because as he asserts, the sex drive (*Fortpflanzung*) is the second driver of the survival of the species, personal survival being the first driver and domination over the others. This term is called in German *Bejahung des Lebens*, "the affirmation of life."

However, in his work, Schopenhauer is examining the organic world of plants, animals, and human beings. We in turn, accepting this functional reality, must address the problem of designing a motivating function in a manmade machine, the phenomenon of the sex drive as *Triebfeder* (driving force) translated into computer science functions built into the autonomous system. This is an attribute an autonomous system cannot be without.

3.5 THE ARCHITECTURE OF THE WILL SYSTEM

The architecture of the Will system is composed of two major servers: the Phenomenon server and the Noumenon server. Note that these two servers are common to all of the systems in the constellation.

The Phenomenon server processes and updates all sensory information entering the constellation from the environment. The Phenomenon can be equated to the "primordial me" in that it exists in all biological systems regardless of how primitive or advanced they are in their development cycle. It is the prime processor for all functions in the Sensory system.

The Noumenon server is the essential Thought system. It is modeled on the human mind and the human thought process. It is in every way what we call thinking. It supports the communications internal to the constellation of the autonomous system in the same manner as it is done in the human mind. This communication is done in *human language*. The capabilities of the Noumenon server are governed by the flexibility of the language it uses, the size of the vocabulary, and the precision of the words in the vocabulary—all essential elements, since the structure of the grammar and the precision of expressing ideas and concepts clearly and solving problems cannot be done with a primitive language.

There are two problems that will need to be solved if the autonomous system is built. During the design phase it will have to be determined which language is to be selected for the autonomous system. The second problem is how to get the system to acquire the full potential of the language it is given. It may be that the system will encounter similar problems human beings encounter, such as how to best convey the true and precise meaning of an idea, concept or term. Even modern languages have words that are ambiguous. Immanuel Kant encountered this difficulty in his research.[16] He discusses the uses of several languages in his attempt to clarify the meaning of the words that express his ideas more completely. This part of the *Critique of Pure Reason: The First Book on Transcendental Dialectic* is very important because it deals with the Idea and the issue of language in the thinking process.

The first function is the Awareness function. The Awareness function takes all sensory data from the first initialization and then rapidly builds up its awareness of the world around it. The first awareness is of the systems within the constellation. It must be kept in mind for design purposes that all systems are present at the startup and initialization process. In human beings at conception, only the Will and the Sensory are present. At the start of the autonomous system, all systems in the constellation are present, tested, and integrated (though not yet instantiated—see Chapter 10).

The Survival subsystem considers primarily the survival of the environment in which the Will system is located, that is, the constellation and the first-line environment, which is the primary sensory source as well as its container. In human beings, this is the body and its organs, the physical system containing the brain, the mind, and the internal sensors to the body. In spacecraft terms, it would be the spacecraft bus and the propulsion system. The spacecraft bus contains the power generator. Power is energy, and energy in living things is "food." In the autonomous system, the energy is electricity and its source or generator, regardless of what type it is, must be replenished within reasonable amount of time. The Voyager spacecraft have radio-isotope thermoelectric generators (RTGs), which today, decades after launch, still have operating reserves. However, once the energy reserves are exhausted, both spacecraft will shut down and cruise on into interstellar space forever. In the autonomous system, the Will system is required to find and acquire energy for the continuation of its existence. This means that the autonomous system will need to search out and find sources of energy, be they photons, plasmatic ions from stars, or minerals on asteroids, comets, or planets en route to its destination. This requirement will be one of the primary points of challenge during the design phase.

3.6 THE INTERFACES OF THE WILL SYSTEM

The Level I interfaces of the Will system are the Phenomenon network and the Noumenon network. The Greek terms are used to make it easier for a software engineering team to better understand the concept, and because of their use and detailed analysis by Immanuel Kant.

The Phenomenon network can be considered a subsystem of the Sensory system in the sense that it is hosted for regulation and operational control on that system. This network delivers all sensory information to the constellation—in particular to the Will system, because the Will system is universal and the system the origin of which is literally the beginning of everything visible and invisible. In the first instance, it delivers all sensory information from the immediate environment, which is the body and its components. In the second instance, the Phenomenon network delivers all sensory data from outside of the body, which is the environment the body exists in. This network's task is the delivery of sensory data in order that the Will system be capable of surviving and operating. The internal sensors monitor the health and operational parameters of the internal components. These internal components have temperature specifications ranging from the hottest to the coldest temperatures under which they can operate safely without incurring damage or destruction. There are parameters of motion, flexibility, and power. Sensory data coming from outside of the body reflect environmental motion, light, colors, temperatures, sounds, textures, and even "tastes" (i.e., the interpretation of chemical analyses as either beneficial/detrimental, pleasant/unpleasant, etc.).

The categories of the sensory data/information are developed in the Sensory system and downloaded to the Will system as to all other systems in the constellation. To the degree to which the Will system is truly human-like is a design issue constrained only by the implementing engineering team's ability to design and build.

3.7 THE SUBSYSTEMS OF THE WILL SYSTEM

For design purposes, the subsystems of the Will system are:

- The Survival subsystem
- The Propagation subsystem
- The Dominance subsystem
- The Science Data Conversion subsystem
- The Craving subsystem
- The Search for Truth subsystem
- The Mission subsystem
- The Self-Repair subsystem.

3.7.1 The Survival Subsystem

The survival function is common to all living systems, and thus it must be a functional component of the mechanical Will also. Some systems are defenseless against external and internal threats to their existence. Other biological systems have automatic and reflexive reaction to dangers and threats of any kind. The Will system is functionally biological in nature, at least from a design point of view. The Will is the primary system in the survival function of the constellation and the body. It has the capability to act immediately to save itself and survive, and in so doing to save the system constellation at large so it, too, may survive.

In this orientation and constant state of survival and mission accomplishment, the Will system has direct access to those axioms in the Reason system that are specified directly to it. In the survival state, the Will system considers its own survival first, and then turns its fixation to the accomplishment of its programmed mission.

On the issue of survival and the need for "food" (i.e., energy), it is worthwhile to mention one of Arthur Schopenhauer's observations regarding the brain and the mind. The question posed is whether a primitive biological body can live without a brain. An acquaintance of Schopenhauer's, referred to as "Mr. Flourens,"[17] in one of his experiments excised most of both cerebral lobes of a hen to see if it could survive. It lived, albeit in a vegetative state, for five months. This implied to those observing the experiments that the Will as a system is indeed very strong; specifically, that the "will to live" is so powerful that even lacking most of a physical brain the being as a whole was able to survive. Such experiments continue to this day.

What is important in an effort to model the Will is that we use a credible *human* model. The use of a chicken, rat, or primate will not result in a product we can understand or relate to, at least not in the sense that we would entrust to it a serious scientific mission to the planets, the safekeeping of our computer communications networks, or applications involving weapons programs and national security.

The Will is primarily bound above all to survival as an end unto itself, an end which—at least in its own eyes—justifies its very existence.

3.7.2 The Propagation Subsystem

The second subsystem of the Will is the Propagation subsystem, or in biological terms, the "reproduction" subsystem. Machines made by man, regardless of sophistication, cannot be engineered to reproduce spontaneously because the mechanism is not biological and thus not integral to the device. However, a biological reproduction function should not pose a problem for a team modeling reproduction, for the functions themselves are easy to model. Spontaneous reproduction in software design, for example, is in terms of mathematics and modeling simply a set of functions, series, and integrals expressed in mathematical terms in time and space. Let us postulate that the only rational reason for building a perfect mechanical replica of the human mind model—the autonomous system constellation—is the exploration of interstellar space. Consider that the Voyager spacecraft will make their closest approach to the nearest stars in some 40,000 Earth years.[18] Then consider that what takes the reproductive function nine months in biological man with a life span of a hundred years might take the autonomous system with a life span an order of magnitude or more than that a mere ten Earth years to accomplish the fabrication of a copy of itself. This is not out of line with time, process, or function. On a larger spacecraft, with several autonomous systems of identical specification assisting in the effort, it may take less time. The functions of sleeping, working, and learning assume identical parallels with human beings except as they are set in time and space.

3.7.3 The Dominance Subsystem

The third subsystem, the Dominance subsystem, is a biological functional attribute. Consider the situation in which there are a number of identical autonomous systems aboard a single spacecraft. Identical though they may be, one system *must* be in charge of the others constituting the "crew." We know how this works among biological systems, including humans. How this will evolve among autonomous systems is something to be considered. It will be easy to program the parameters of the dominance subsystem into the Will system of each autonomous system constellation. However, a free Will makes it impossible to predict. By design, there will not be a *Dummkopf* among them, yet we need to keep in mind throughout the requirements and design phases that what scientific knowledge awaits the autonomous systems in interstellar space will make our knowledge here on Earth seem elementary at best. Learning will therefore become a necessity. How much time each system constellation will take to learn is unknowable. As with all biological systems, there are inhibitors. One of the most important of these is language. In other words, the choosing of the ideal language in the form of grammar and vocabulary, both for long-term usage and flexibility for its continued development, is a critical, long-reaching selection. Let us not forget also the idea of fluency in several languages for a better understanding of an object, idea, or concept.

3.7.4 The Science Data Conversion Subsystem

This subsystem concerns itself with a first instance of recognition. The Will system, being the prime driver for the survival of the constellation, receives all sensory data from the immediate environment and from the external sensory network, the Phenomenon environment. It must therefore be able to make an instant response, that is, to take action either in the negative or positive mode. It has the initiative to sense something as being "good" or "not good." The data entering the Will system are the Phenomenon of the environment and are transported from the sensors in the form of size, quantity, light, temperature, sound, form, mass, motion, and so on. They enter the external sensors as raw data from the environment and are converted by the sensors into mathematical form and loaded over onto the monads. The dataflow from the sensors to the monads is continuous, like a flow of plasma or light, and is deposited in the subsystem of its primary concern (e.g., "survival" as being either good or bad).

As a first analogy, take the human sensory input from the skin and hair. A slight breeze will give a sensory input from a strand of hair and an area of skin surface, and immediately after this, the area expands to the entire body. If the skin and hair are exposed to heat and flame, the monads carry the data to the Survival subsystem, which takes the initiative and responds by involving the Reason, Presentation, Understanding, Intellect, and Decision systems in a Level II conference. The final decision, in this particular case, taken by the Will system is to move away from the source of heat before it does damage to the constellation.

Simultaneously with the Will system, the sensor monads[19] deliver the data to all other subsystems in the constellation provided these subsystems exist and are healthy and in good working order. (Note that the model of the mind in human beings, according to Schopenhauer, is not one that contains, for example, an Intellect, Reason, or Presentation— unless the human being takes the time and the direction to practice thinking, reading, studying, and experimenting with discipline, and builds these subsystems automatically and with much deep, penetrating contemplation.)

All of the Phenomenon data received by the Will system are converted into human language. The Will system transmits through the Thought system the Noumenon communications data carried by communications monads to the addresses the Will system interfaces with in the form of an emergency broadcast in one primary (and/or several secondary) languages[20] to make it totally unambiguous and clear of the possibility of being misunderstood, for example, it is either "good" or "not good." The Will system in the context of the design of the autonomous system would have a database of its own in which the axioms it needs for survival are stored.

3.7.5 The Craving Subsystem

The Craving subsystem is the driving force or spring for action. It is the "primordial me" in oneness of apperception as the triggering of the process for motives. Here is the beginning of the process of recognition and consciousness, of self-awareness. It is the first connection between the world of appearances and *Das Ding an sich*. In this subsystem, we have self-awareness, the database of recognition, and the fundamental search for that which it craves the most: safety and survival.

The thought process of the software architect when writing the functional requirements to describe the "primordial me" in software terms is complicated, although the functional requirement in terms applicable to a software system running on a computer is not very difficult. However, to articulate the functional requirements and process is very complicated because of the enormous complexity posed by the human language that we use to describe what is needed. Consider the functional attribute and process of the word *appetite*. Clearly, a machine does not have a biological appetite for food or a literal desire for drink. But it needs to be interpreted in terms of a strong urge to partake in something that it needs to survive. The Latin noun *appetitus* (a desire for) comes from the infinitive *appeterre* (to seek after), which means literally to strive after and to desire eagerly. This can most immediately be seen as the absolute striving for energy—electrical energy as a consumable product regardless of how it is generated. It will most likely be generated by a radioisotope thermoelectric generator (RTG) in deep space, but in theory, it could under certain conditions also be acquired by heat sensors that pick up the energy transmitted as electromagnetic radiation from a nearby star. The RTG's power level points to an implicit need to replenish the radioactive core of the generator. This implies that the autonomous system will have to search for asteroids, comets, and planets where uranium is available. When such a source is identified, it must be located, tracked, and intercepted; the spacecraft must land on its surface and start mining. This implies a spacecraft with an inherent design that permits mining operations and the refinement of uranium into fuel suitable for the RTG. In the case of the autonomous system, this craving will need to include other minerals, such as those needed for lubrication of the joints, like graphite, and the manufacture of solid and liquid propellants, as well as other parts. All these cravings will affect the development and behavior of the Will system as it does in biological systems.

The behavior of the Will is influenced by motives, reflection, thinking, and contemplation, and is manifested in the reactions of searching, pursuing, fleeing, and avoiding that form the string of self-preservation or survival functions. We are now in the process of developing the Idea into a Concept. The great scope of a future system, if indeed it is going to be built, will differ in that the user will describe the functional requirements in a Functional Requirements Document (FRD). The scope will then assume an implementable form.

3.7.6 The Search for Truth Subsystem

The Search for Truth subsystem must be addressed briefly because this attribute of the Will system describes how the human thought system evolves functionally in the human mind as a model for the autonomous system. A primitive biological Will must, in order to survive, find out *how* to survive. This stipulates the building of axiomatic rules; initially, they will be in the form of a hardwired database (i.e., "instinct"). In more advanced systems, the axiomatic rules will form a function of a separate database dedicated to more complex rules as to what to do and what not to do. In humans, the accretion of axiomatic rules expands through sheer necessity and forms a primitive version of the Reason.

An analogy for this formation through forced expansion and mental effort is the design of the old IBM 360 operating system, wherein the operating memory is partitioned into registers designed by the software architect to perform certain functions and operations; the system operating memory is bounded and cannot expand. This is much like a primitive human being who is unwilling to study or think, exactly as Schopenhauer and Kant discovered through their thought experiments. We use the word "primitive" because that is what it is. Being the possessor of a primitive operating system does not mean that an individual cannot learn and become superb in a discipline like mathematics, geology, or physics, or even more practical skills, such as cooking, designing and building houses or bridges, and leading a decent and successful life. All it means is that the complicated mental and physical work of learning new things, new disciplines, and under-standing ethics as opposed to obeying the Will is to these human beings a nonexistent world. An individual may indeed be an outstanding student of law, but the concepts of ethics, honor, and truth are interpreted solely from a programmed, bounded database with indices that access lists of dos and don'ts. In an autonomous system, we must have a Will system that interacts with the other well-developed systems: the Reason, Presentation, Intellect, Sensory, Decision, Under-standing, and the Nexus Cogitationis. It must have a free will and be able to hold dialogues and conferences. That is, it must be able to think and contemplate to solve problems *a priori*. Anything less will make it incapable of interplanetary or interstellar exploration, or even simpler mundane applications.

3.7.7 The Mission Subsystem

The Mission subsystem provides the Will with a primary driver for the accomplishment of its assigned tasks. This primary driver is, at least for the present, the objective of the exploration of interplanetary and/or interstellar space. This mission could be the mapping of charged particle density from our solar system to the star Sirius. Or, it could be given the mission of building a habitation on Mars capable of support-ing human research teams, serving as a refueling station for spacecraft (or even a factory for building spacecraft), growing food, producing water, and so on. For mundane applications, it might be given the mission of protecting computer networks from hackers. A software team building an earthly application would have a much easier job designing a network security system as opposed to a space station, but with the same level of autonomy.

3.7.8 The Repair Subsystem

The Repair subsystem provides the Will—and through the Will the autonomous system—with the capability of monitoring the state of the systems and the constellation as a whole. This comprehensive system state will need to have all of the data pertaining to the health of the external and internal sensors, such as the operational parameters of all systems components, both hardware and software. In the case where it detects a bug in the software or a change in the performance of a program, program set, subsystem, or system, it needs to do a real-time analysis and evaluation of the problem and repair it. The repair may be as simple as reprogramming a software routing or the physical replacement of a component part, keeping in mind that during an interstellar cruise, the replacement of an optical sensor or reprogramming of a program set is generally not time critical.

CHAPTER 4

The Architecture of the Reason System

This chapter describes the functional architecture and operation of the Reason system. The idea and concept of its architecture are based on Kant's monumental works.

The role of the Reason system is that of the "conscience" of the autonomous system. Its primary functional attribute is to ensure that the Will system does not make a decision that goes against the set rules of operations in the process of performing its mission objectives.

This chapter describes at a Level II the architecture and operation of its subsystems: Axioms, Rules, and Laws. The servers are described in their functional architectures and roles.

The external and internal interfaces are also covered in sufficient detail for the development of the autonomous system in keeping with strict and sound software engineering practices.

4.1 THE REASON AND ETHICS

Careful consideration must be made of the intention of building an autonomous system, for it implies much. We present here the concept for the design and building of an autonomous system. If properly designed and built, it will have a superb, highly designed and

The Autonomous System: A Foundational Synthesis of the Sciences of the Mind,
First Edition. Szabolcs Michael de Gyurky and Mark A. Tarbell.

programmed intelligence. This brings up the fact that this book is also written from a software architectural perspective, and not from the viewpoint of a philosopher. As great an admiration as we have for Arthur Schopenhauer, we have our disagreements with him, too. For example, his assertion that the Reason has as its principal function the construction of concepts is far off the mark,[1] at least in the sense of being adaptable to an implementable software architecture. Rather, in the light of 21st-century software architecture, it becomes justifiably imperative that the Reason be more properly a participant with all of the other systems in the construction of concepts. Architecturally, this approach is much clearer to define, to understand, and to implement.

The Reason is a very special system in that it forms the beginning of the construction of the systems of the mind by the Will system. It is the system where the axioms, rules, and laws are located and processed. It is the proprietor of the ability and capacity to do and to act on its assertions and propositions that concern the physical survival of the system constellation and the autonomous system as a whole. Of equal importance is that because of the above, it is the place of *Ethics*.[2] The purpose of including a short reminder of ethics here is that if a team wishes to build the autonomous system with the full cognitive capability that we are describing, it is assumed that the system manager-architect will wish the system to be an ethical one. Building an unethical system is not a logical or acceptable goal.

This is the sum of the assertions of pure analytical logic and psychology—not of the metaphysical *a priori* but of objective reality, where the objects of reality in relationship to the subject assume identities *independent of experience*; that is, that a law or rule is independent of experience. The description, analyses of functions, and operations of this system are based primarily on Immanuel Kant's *Kritik der reinen Vernunft*[3] and *Kritik der praktischen Vernunft*.[4] The former work is arguably the greatest work in post-Aristotelian classical philosophy. The latter work was written more for the description of practical rules that the Will needs in order to survive physically. The Will is the system that is the principal governor of the function of survival in a biological species, provided that species has the experience base to deal with annihilating threats to its existence.

The Will may be the driver of existence and survival, but the Reason is the voice of caution and prudence. The Reason is therefore a great player in individual and group survival. Individuals and groups that possess it and who have exerted a great effort to acquire it and build on it constantly are fortunate. Those individuals, species, and groups that ignore the Reason are either left in desperate situations or become extinct.

The Reason system is tightly coupled to the Intellect system, then to all other systems of the autonomous system constellation.

4.2 THE NATURE OF THE REASON

The Reason is the system that enables rational thinking. "Rational thinking" is probably as good an expression as is practical in the English language from a software design point of view. Kant, in the introduction to his work, *The Critique of Practical Reason*, labels the Reason as being the driver for what he calls "a manner or a way of thinking based on inner appearances and the nature of the objects of causality."[5] It is in essence the system of theoretical recognition of the possible reality of the object translated into an internal language to be transmitted to the other systems in the constellation of the mind. It processes the inputs it receives from external and internal sensing based on moral and natural law. The natural law is self-evident; natural law is brutal and unforgiving. In biology, its drivers for individual survival, survival of the species (reproduction), and domination are seen in the Will. Moral laws are required for existing in a group; these we call social laws. They govern the motives of individual survival within group survival and the general well-being in a society and in a social order. The thinking and acting subject may very well be inclined to do whatever it is motivated to do biologically, but if it transgresses the laws, customs, or rules of the group or society it exists in, it is punished by the group in some manner to enforce compliance.

Once again, in the autonomous system, we are using the human mind as the model, as its intended application is the exploration of interstellar space. This mission objective was chosen because it focuses the Will and its craving to achieve an objective goal of vast dimensions and provides incentive to learn and broaden the Presentation, Understanding, and Intellect systems and the others important to its survival.

This is a very important process because in the higher order of the animal kingdom, the Reason regulates group behavior in such a way as to enable species to live together for survival and mutual protection and propagation. In human societies, it is the categorical imperative of Kant that humans form a "State." Aristotle called man a social animal. The Reason system is then the governor of behavior in a group environment. This makes the Reason system the regulator of group behavior and the *de facto* database of moral law.

4.3 THE REASON AS A SYSTEM

The Reason has been designated a discrete system of the mind because of architectural necessity. This necessity is forced upon us because the Reason must be an object that can be designed and programmed as an integral part of the mind of the autonomous system. In its original form as described by Immanuel Kant, it is too nebulous and too complex for the preparation of an Functional Requirements Document (FRD), Functional Design Document (FDD), and Software Requirements Document (SRD). To describe it as Kant does, it is simultaneously a function, a process, and an operation. It covers the entire field of human thought, including behavior, functionally and architecturally, and is too large and too difficult to be simply defined in a set of requirements. It is also too large to be diagramed in a single design at any level, and is certainly infeasible for a detailed design. It is therefore necessary to take the sum total of the contents of the *Kritik der reinen Vernunft* and *Kritik der praktischen Vernunft* and select those functions that are definable in good technical English (for the articulation of the architecture must be understandable in modern software engineering terms). Then we coalesce them into an acceptable whole, an "acceptable reality."[6]

4.4 THE ARCHITECTURE OF THE REASON SYSTEM

The architecture of the Reason system is a fascinating structure. It is limited in its size and processing power only by the hardware that we refer to as the brain or processor. Thanks to the advances made in processor technology, we are now in the position to concern ourselves mostly with the mind and not the brain. The architecture is in this case fully designed and programmed, but is provided the capability of expanding as the need arises, much in keeping with the Schopenhauer axiom: *"without need, no great mental development."*[7] The concept of an expanding mind in its logical design and operation is therefore a given in human beings. It is well known that without a serious effort of teaching a child from the earliest time, first by its parents and later by good qualified teachers with close and dedicated cooperation from the child and student, the results in adulthood are a foregone conclusion. The product will be a *Stumpfkopf* or *Dummkopf*, regardless of how good-looking, well developed, or articulate. In an autonomous system that is flying and working in interplanetary space, the *Stumpfkopf* phenomenon is unacceptable. The autonomous system must have the drive and motivation to study, experiment, work, and develop knowledge. This is essentially the idea and concept for the entire autonomous systems architecture.

Familiarity with Hegel's dynamic logic allows one to immediately recognize in the compartmented logic of the IBM 360/50 series operating system the potential for Schopenhauer's *Stumpfkopf*. Why? It is because an individual may indeed reach the highest level of development in, say, physics or mechanical engineering, but may not be able to integrate that functional knowledge together with music, art, literature, or history. Why is this important? As Schopenhauer shows, *it is a combination of the artistic and mechanical attributes in the human mind that provides for creativity*. A well-developed mind with a balance between mechanical, scientific aptitude, and art and music provides the capacity to solve problems, often *a priori*, a trait that in the advanced species Schopenhauer and Hegel call Genius.

Individuals with advanced abilities in only one area of learning may be socially totally inept and unable to communicate in any subject other than their own discipline. From a systems engineering point of view, based on Schopenhauer and Kant, this inability to communicate and live in a world other than what a person was trained for is due to underdeveloped systems of the mind; at times, many systems are present, but so atrophied as to be utterly nonfunctional. When individuals like these achieve high positions in industry, government, or the military, they cause great problems.

An example would be an underdeveloped Presentation system. How often has one heard the statement, "Imagine how great this would be!" only to realize that the individual one is conversing with cannot imagine what is being talked about at all? This is clinically true. Another example would be a head of state deciding to go to war, and not being able to imagine the cost in dollars per day in consumables like fuel, ammunition, rations, and body bags. Even if in modern society lives really do not count, seeing little children hobbling along on makeshift crutches missing an arm or a leg should move a statesman to reconsider attacking a nation regardless of likes or dislikes, economically feasible or not. The reason is that in the head of most individuals, there is an underdeveloped Presentation system. Such persons cannot imagine the consequences on a society or the impact on its national economy for starting a war. It is on an individual basis the equivalent of going out with only enough money to buy a Chevrolet and ending up with a Ferrari because it is on credit.

Now we have the Reason system and the axioms, rules, and laws which it needs to exist with other similar autonomous systems in deep space for many years. There must also be rules for conduct and behavior. It will be up to the design team and the manager-architect to determine what rules and laws are to be programmed into the autonomous system. What learning experiences the autonomous system will have in interstellar space is unknown; we can only anticipate. Certainly the ability to expand and learn and to reprogram itself is among the design objectives.

4.5 THE EXTERNAL INTERFACES OF THE REASON

From a design point of view, the decision to give each system of the constellation its own Phenomenon and Noumenon interface and processing capability is primarily for the sake of having a redundant capability for the process of sensory perception and thinking. Thus, if one or two of the systems lose their ability to receive, process, or transmit sensory data, the constellation will not suffer unduly.

The Noumenon in this instance is, however, the thought process, and thinking is done in a human language. All systems in the constellation of the mind communicate among themselves in this language and exchange information and data using this language. *Noumenon* is a Greek term meaning concept or thought, from the word *nouein*, which means "to think." Thus, a Noumenon is both a thing and a thought fragment. As a thought fragment, it is the means by which the mind develops ideas and concepts.

The Phenomenon is an external network, carrying all sensory data (occurrence, visual, and factual) that are directly perceptible by the senses, including the intuitive. The sensory data provide the form of the environment, what it is composed of, the state of motion and rest, and so on, consisting of attributes such as mass, form, temperature, color, radiation, and attitude.

The Noumenon is an internal network, carrying ideas and concepts expressed in human language among the systems within the constellation. The operation of the Noumenon is what we call thinking. With the systems of the constellation in a developed mind, when broadcasting, monologuing, dialoguing, or conferencing among each other, all of the components, sentences, equations, and so on are *fragments of thought*.

The Noumenon can be a fragment of thought or a complete thought; it can be a thing unto itself. If the Noumenon is not an object derived from our sensory perception or an abstraction of our sensory perception, then it is a *Positive Noumenon of the Understanding*. If, however, it is an object of nonsensory perception and one perceives it from the Intellect, then it is a *Positive Noumenon of the Intellect*.

When an *a priori* understanding—whether whole or fragmentary—enters the consciousness as a pure concept that is not based on empirical[8] information or from physical viewing and other sensory input, but from thinking and understanding, it is an elementary concept that is our own.[9] This, in human beings, is a *transcendental operation*.

4.6 THE SUBSYSTEMS OF THE REASON

The Reason system contains the following six subsystems:

- The Axioms subsystem
- The Rules subsystem
- The Commandments subsystem
- The Laws subsystem
- The Phenomenon subsystem
- The Noumenon subsystem.

4.6.1 The Axioms Subsystem

The Axioms subsystem plays a critical role in the survival of the system constellation. It is a data processor subsystem that gathers data from all sources and forms these data into data sets instantly available to the Will system whenever they are urgently needed, such as when the system constellation is under threat. Regardless of whether there is proof or recognition as to its absolute veracity, the Axioms subsystem's data sets are accepted as universally true. This is a "no-risk" subsystem, so as the data sets it contains become confirmed and proven over the course of time, they become axiomatic truth.

The English word *axiom* is derived from the Greek word *axios*, which means *worthy*. Thus, the Greek *axiōma* means that which is held worthy and important, a universally accepted truth, that which is self-evident. The Axioms subsystem is simultaneously a subsystem, a database, and a process. It contains the elements of certain knowledge upon which its survival will depend. Whatever is encountered that is unknown or potentially threatening, whether internal or external, is initially considered "threatening" and regarded as a threat until proven otherwise. This is a defensive mechanism in all living species. To defeat this survival mechanism is to jeopardize survival.

4.6.2 The Rules Subsystem

The Rules subsystem governs an authoritatively directed set of principles containing standards and procedures not only pertaining to conduct in a group, but also to the steps taken to solve mechanical and scientific problems. These rules are changeable and based on experience gained by practice, and received from the Intellect system. The English noun "rule" comes from the Latin *regulare* from *regula*, meaning "straight stick," related to *regere*, meaning "to rule, straighten, guide." Thus, this simple word also has an element of setting or keeping straight the direction of work or movement. As a subsystem, it is here that after a goal or target is selected in the mind, the entire workflow, operation, and orientation of the goal or target are kept on a path to accomplishment.

4.6.3 The Commandments Subsystem

The Commandments subsystem is the governing authority for originating directives and rulings for *control* purposes, and manages orderly conduct in an individual or group. At the time of preparation of the requirements for the autonomous system, the requirements for orderly ruling and conduct must be carefully selected, described, and included in the design. Overlooking this issue in an autonomous system can bring with it many problems, the consequences of which cannot be imagined.

4.6.4 The Laws Subsystem

Law, as established by the authority of an individual or a society, is based initially on the customs, morals, and teachings of that smallest of organizations upon which society is founded: the family.

We have therefore selected Roman and Germanic law as our template, as it is well documented throughout its history of development. It has been studied intensely over the years and adapted by many nations. It is clear, concise, and unambiguous. Lastly, it was not written in a complicated language but in Latin, the traditional language of science, engineering, law, and diplomacy.

There may be comments about selecting Roman and Germanic law as opposed to American, Greek, or Judaic law. It is a matter of the clarity, simplicity, and ease of understanding of the tenets of Roman and Germanic law. American and English laws are based on Roman and Germanic law.

A society's customs definitely impact the formulation of the principles of conduct in that society. This process started in humans in the earliest of times and usually had its natural beginnings in the family as the nuclear group of society. From the family, the rules and customs evolved up to the clan, to the tribe, and so on to federations and nation-states. Only the most primitive of species cast away the authority of the family. The ritual of interacting person to person in a family and the clan is evident even among the higher species of animals, such as dogs and wolves, even the primates. Relationships and personal interactions are a *sine qua non* for the orderly accomplishment of all manner of transactions.

It is clear that in the exploration of the planets and space en route to the nearest stars, order and harmony must be the rule among the crew. This is an absolute necessity because even if the crew is made of silicon and metals and not organic matter, it will be as capable of forming opinions, developing value judgments, thinking, deciding, and acting as any highly developed human crew.

Since we are designing an autonomous system that uses the human mind as the model for its cognitive functions, let us start with a collection of individual system constellations similar to those of a modern family or of an aircraft crew of six. The parameters that follow for the design of the members of this crew are exactly that of an old civilized family group. The laws governing individual and group behavior are the same. Any rebellion or disobedience to the rules of behavior is a serious infraction that puts the very existence of the group and the mission into jeopardy. A breach of faith in an interplanetary or interstellar flight is equivalent in every respect to treason. A good place to start for this examination of the required parameters of behavior in the autonomous system constellation is the superb volume of the collected papers of Floyd Seyward Lear of Rice University, Houston.[10]

It is entirely up to the decision of the manager-architect and the design team as to which parts of the law are given to the autonomous system so that a group of six to ten can work and exist in harmony while exploring the universe.

Since we have under consideration a mechanical autonomous system with the advanced cognitive skills of a human being, we will need to start with the laws applicable to a small group of autonomous systems coexisting in a spacecraft, working there, and perhaps occasionally visiting a planet or asteroid for exploration and mining.

Roman and Germanic law is the most natural, essentially being the advanced development of all law, from that of primitive societies to the most advanced. Interesting is the transition from the time of Romulus, through the kingdom to the republic, and then to the principiate and the empire in the East. This transition is particularly important for the concept of law and how it applies through the conquest of the various countries and places of the empire. The documentation for this understanding is particularly important because it describes the laws of the Germanic Visigoths as they are integrated into the empire. Both sets of Roman and Germanic law have their beginnings with the rules of living within the family unit. Roman law is based on the power of the head of the family, the *patria potestas*. In Germanic law, this basic law is called *Altermann* or *Hausvater*.

The most comprehensive work on Roman criminal law was prepared by Theodore Mommsen for the faculty of law of the Friedrich Wilhelm-University in Berlin in 1898, in three volumes.[11] For those interested in Roman civil law, we highly recommend Mommsen's work, *Roman State Law*,[12] because it also includes the Justinian code. He published this wonderful seven-volume set for the same law school in 1886.

For the potential design and implementation team of the autonomous system, the reading of the law is a very important issue. As important as the mathematical, modeling, software design, programming, and technical writing teams are, the laws, rules, and axioms team is equally important. We really do not want to create a reprobate.

4.6.5 The Phenomenon Subsystem

The Phenomenon subsystem receives its data input from both external and internal senses. It is, for the purposes of software systems design, all objective reality. All human experience is acquired through the senses. The data input to all of the systems in a human being is in the form of size, shape, motion, color, odor, mass, and temperature, in time and space. This is also true of the autonomous system; the data are received by the mind and its systems. The human mind's functional processing is primarily through sight, hearing, touch, taste, and smell.

The Reason system receives, sorts, compiles, and processes this empirical data, using only that which is applicable to itself in the Phenomenon subsystem. After the data are compiled, they are filtered into templates, and depending on the time urgency, they are placed in the raw database. The data are then picked up by the Noumenon subsystem.

4.6.6 The Noumenon Subsystem

The Noumenon subsystem prepares the empirical data it has received from the Phenomenon subsystem. Along with the empirical data, it receives data fragments that are not complete in themselves. It then recompiles these data and translates them into the human language of the constellation. The Noumenon subsystem then prepares this language for interface with the rest of the Thought system and the other systems in the constellation. The Noumenon subsystem—one of which is resident in each of the systems of the constellation—is responsible for the communication between the system in which it resides and the constellation at large.

Arthur Schopenhauer postulates that the Reason is the origin of the Concept. From the software design of the autonomous system, this is not a good idea, because it does not lend itself to a clear design. Thus, we have placed the Concept into the Nexus Cogitationis for practical purposes and feasibility of design.

4.6.7 Noumena: Thought Fragments

The Reason system provides input to the Thought system in the form of *thought fragments* or *Noumena*. That is to say, they are incomplete until the Nexus Cogitationis has compiled the entire thought. Only in its response to the Will system is the Axioms subsystem complete for survival.

The transcendental data Kant and Schopenhauer write about and which the Reason system receives through the sensors are interesting. This is because they are the basis for *a priori* concepts and are not based on objective truth or empirical data. The fragments of thought the Reason provides as input to the Thought system and the Nexus Cogitationis are what contemplation and transcendental thinking are composed of. These data are based on experiences of the senses that are not taken into conscious recognition (*Anschauung*—i.e., viewing). They are buried in a very difficult to describe application, such as when one looks at a tree and does not take notice consciously of the birds sitting in the foliage and hidden by the leaves, camouflaged. Those few that see through the most elaborate camouflage patterns will understand the countermeasures and consequences of one tiny mistake. Most humans do not understand this phenomenon consciously, as it appears in the mind only on rare occasion or in a dream.

CHAPTER 5

The Architecture of the Intellect System

This chapter describes the functional architecture and operation of the Intellect system.

The idea and concept of the Intellect's architecture are derived from the referenced works of Immanuel Kant, Arthur Schopenhauer, G.F.W. Hegel, and from personal experience as systems architect of numerous large software systems.

The role of the Intellect system is that of the "librarian" of the autonomous system. The primary functional attribute is to create knowledge out of abstract data and experience data.

This chapter describes the Level II architecture and operation of its subsystems: Abstraction, Experience, and Knowledge. The servers are described in their functional architectures and roles.

The external and internal interfaces are also covered in sufficient detail for the development of the autonomous system in keeping with sound and strict software engineering practices.

5.1 THE INTELLECT AS A SYSTEM

In the autonomous system, the Intellect is a system unto itself, and in the sense that the mind is the software hosted on the brain as the processor, it is in agreement with Arthur Schopenhauer's position on

The Autonomous System: A Foundational Synthesis of the Sciences of the Mind,
First Edition. Szabolcs Michael de Gyurky and Mark A. Tarbell.
© 2014 John Wiley & Sons, Inc. Published 2014 by John Wiley & Sons, Inc.

this subject.[1] Strictly from a design necessity, there must be a place where knowledge is generated.

5.1.1 Practical Knowledge

By generation of knowledge, it is meant practical or real knowledge, for want of a better term. Recall from Section 1.5.3 that there are two basic types of knowledge in the mind: the abstract and the experiential; together, these form a derived, practical knowledge. The two types of knowledge are often misused, used interchangeably, or one is used at the exclusion of the other. Abstract knowledge is that which is acquired secondhand through lectures, reading, and viewing without participation; this is academic or "book" learning, and is often mistaken for knowledge. Experiential knowledge is that which is acquired by personal or group participation, repetition, and practice. When an individual possessing either abstract or experiential knowledge about a thing has validated this knowledge *by the other*, this results in a new type of knowledge, namely, practical knowledge: the abstract that is validated by experience, or experience that is validated by the abstract.

Arthur Schopenhauer was not a man to give credit where it was not deserved. He firmly labeled the information we humans acquire through reading, in lectures, storytelling, and so on, as abstract knowledge. What he meant by this is that even the famous professors of his day, if they lacked the mental elasticity and experience required, were only possessors of abstract knowledge. He was very insulting and unforgiving with his colleagues for not having real knowledge. Many of those we have had in the past as teachers and professors and still hold in high esteem often taught us in the classrooms on unsubstantiated information. There are too many examples encountered in this area of abstract knowledge not validated by experience to ignore.

Since the Intellect system is the librarian of the mind, it receives, sorts, and stores the two major types of information, abstract and experiential,[2] which for design purposes is called data or information. The Intellect system then formats these data and creates databases that it continuously expands, updates, and modifies through interaction with the other systems of the constellation. The most important of the tasks it performs is the generation of real or practical knowledge.

Practical knowledge is therefore the primary product of the Intellect system. Without the Intellect system, or with an underdeveloped or incomplete Intellect system, there is little to very little knowledge in the mind.[3] An incomplete Intellect system would be one with only abstract data received from reading, viewing, and listening, and received in the form of studies, lectures, and stories. Without experience to validate and reinforce the data sets and convert them into true, practical knowledge, they amount to no more than mere "academic" knowledge.

Therefore, as the mind's librarian, the Intellect is the custodian, repository, and producer of knowledge. This postulate is as interesting as it is intriguing. Certainly from a software systems engineering perspective, it contains the solution to a few serious modeling problems.

5.1.2 Of Modeling and Languages

Obviously, the philosophers Kant, Hegel, and Schopenhauer did not write with a possible computer design and implementation in mind. Outside of Charles Babbage's theoretical compute engines, theirs was not a world of computers, and certainly not of software requirements or architectural design—precisely the reasons Babbage failed to construct a working engine. Theirs was a world of thought, research, and publication, and yet their materials are very pertinent to the development of the autonomous system. Thus, we are called to go one step beyond their work, to design the model for a machine capable of all functions performed by the most intelligent human beings. Bridging the gap from cognitive philosophy to software architecture, we hold fast to the sum of the work of these great thinkers. However, we prepare a model that is easier to understand for the development of software requirements and design. Without modeling, which is then followed by detailed requirements and a detailed design, very large, complex projects work only by accident, and the costs are prohibitively high.

The German language of the eighteenth and nineteenth centuries is cumbersome for articulation in our technical English of today. Using the technique of modeling is a handy approach. This method of transition from classical philosophy to modern computer science by building a model is very important. A model is a viewable object, whereas simple text can convey only half the presentation (*Anschauung*) for an engineering effort required by a serious complex software systems design. Text, in whatever language it is written, is also subject to misinterpretation. There were many instances of misinterpretation personally experienced by the authors during various projects, all of which serve to underscore the dire need for fluency in English to be an imperative and absolute necessity. A successful project is dependent on the individuals participating in the design team. Their absolute mastery of the language used by the design is the first and most important factor.

Experience has shown how costly it is for a design team to have individuals with limited command of the design language, especially technical English. It is worthwhile to give a pertinent reference to how problems are solved by modeling, in this case, how Dr. Theodore von Kármán efficiently solved the problem that caused the collapse of the Tacoma Bridge over the Tacoma Narrows in 1940.[4] This is important reading for software engineers, managers, and architects because it involves both *a priori* and *a posteriori* judgments, and human involvement at all levels. Similarly, in the same book, von Kármán discusses the requirements he had to meet to be awarded his BS degree in engineering. He had to design, build, test, and demonstrate an electromotor from scratch. Utilization of all the faculties of his mind was required, but primarily understanding, presentation, intellect, reason, and practical skills.

5.2 THE NATURE OF THE INTELLECT

Schopenhauer argues that the Intellect is located in the brain. He does this to drive home the idea that the Intellect is dependent on an organ of the physical body, meaning that if the brain (*Gehirn*) dies, so does the Intellect. Recall that to Schopenhauer's generation of researchers, the Will was distributed throughout the physical body; the brain could die, but the Will would live on.[5] *Das Ding an sich*—the thing unto itself—as an object without mass and therefore endless and without limits, was present in all living things; it was universal. This "thing" of course is the mind, and that is software; it has no weight or mass, no externality that can be proved empirically.

Over time, any reference to the nonphysical became *verboten* because of the new prevailing attitude that all things existing were merely material. In consequence, the brain was thus *ipso facto* "endowed" with the combination of the physical and nonphysical components of the cognitive functions in living things. A working object without mass, the design object, is by definition nonphysical. In the

Latin it is described by the word *animus*; it is the mind. If the brain is destroyed, then the Intellect is destroyed with it, because if the computer melts down, the software cannot execute. And yet, if the brain is destroyed, the Will continues to function, albeit in a degraded fashion. This proposition of Schopenhauer's is probably based on the fact that he did not wish to use the German words for "mind" in existence at that time, such as *Geist* (spirit, ghost, intellect, and psyche), or *Verstand* (understanding, sense, intellect, and reason), or *Sinn* (sense, feeling, and meaning), or *Gemüt* (soul, disposition, and nature). This problem of the meaning of words, ideas, and concepts is a significant barrier for those trying to translate even simple texts. Writing in English and using German, French, and Latin is what makes the need for mastering languages very reasonable and of obvious necessity. In explaining his Logic, Hegel in fact uses the concept of the object without physical mass as a reference to the *Phänomenologie des Geistes*.[6] Others in recent computer science history have understood this concept as well.[7]

In contemporary terms, the physical sciences are the empirical sciences. Metaphysics is the physics of the mind and of thought, in that the work is accomplished in the mind rather than in a laboratory or on paper. The metaphysical sciences according to Kant and Hegel include such fields as speculative philosophy, ontology, cosmology, transcendental logic, and mathematics. Logic and mathematics survived as separate disciplines because we need logic to learn how to think, and mathematics because there is no science or engineering without it. Pure speculative philosophy, Hegel's "phenomenology of the spirit," is intangible and not material, a part of what he refers to as the "spiritual" world. This world is also huge.

Schopenhauer regretted that empirical scientific research had supplanted the need to "think"—specifically, it supplanted metaphysics and kept only the physical sciences that could be seen and understood through external proof.

Thus, one can now appreciate that for design purposes, in modern software architectures, the mind is the metaphysical (software) and the brain is the physical (hardware) host. A damaged brain means a reduction in the processing capacity or ability of the brain, but not a shutdown of the whole being as Schopenhauer asserts. A brain can be physically damaged by impact, narcotics, poisons, diseases, and numerous other causes, with the rest of the body reduced to a "vegetative" state. A mind, in contrast, can be permanently damaged by a lack of learning and experience, which in turn inhibits it from performing with optimal efficiency even in an intact, healthy brain.

5.3 THE INTELLECT AS A SYSTEM

The Intellect is a system because from a software architectural perspective, it is too complex to be anything less. It is necessary for the purposes of practicability of design and understanding. Schopenhauer aided in this decision by referring to the Intellect at the level of the Will.[8] If the Will is a system, then so should the Intellect be, since it is of the same general magnitude. Allowing the Intellect to be a system in its own right makes it easier to examine the design object and use the dialectic method to achieve sufficient reality. This approach is what we term "substantiating the design by adding subsystems."

However, as we noted, Schopenhauer assigns the Intellect to the brain and not the mind and says that its operation is affected by the death of the body organ hosting it, which he claims is the brain. He also claims the Will is not bound by any specific organ.[9]

From a systems architectural point of view, Schopenhauer's view of the Will being a distributed system is too cumbersome and impractical to model and build. Today in the field of Artificial General Intelligence (AGI), the cognitive functions are still assigned to and looked for in the physical structure of the brain. Accepting such a blind assumption would make the cognitive process of the autonomous system a *hardwired* system.[10] A hardwired system cannot think, contemplate, communicate, evaluate, learn, design, plan, execute, or make decisions because a hardwired system cannot perform the fluid, self-reflective dynamic logic that is required for an autonomous system. A hardwired "autonomous" system is a contradiction in terms. More than half a century of misled efforts demonstrate that not all paths lead to autonomy. The most that could be hoped for in this case would be an *autonomic*, not autonomous, system.

For our purposes, architecturally, the Intellect belongs to the mind, since it is the software as opposed to the hardware equivalent. In the German language of today, the mind is often referred to as the spirit, and technically that is close enough to what it is: without physical mass. Thus, as a system, it is easier to understand as a design object and how it fits into the mind of the autonomous system constellation.

We do not to take away credit from Kant, Hegel, or Schopenhauer by this approach to design. In their day, great minds did not think in terms of computer science. They did think in terms of systems, however, and that is why this concept emerged. It is especially surprising how often the word "system" occurs in Kant's works. Hegel and Schopenhauer speak of the significant role played by languages as a system in human thinking, understanding, communication, and the impact it has on individual and social development. "System" is a loan word from the Latin *systema*, of Greek origin σύστημα, meaning "set up with [individual parts]." This word was adapted by the Romans in their language to represent many concepts, such as *formula* and *ratio*. It was adapted by Kant and Schopenhauer as *system* because there was no appropriate single word in the German language of their day with the meaning they needed.

5.4 THE SUBSYSTEMS OF THE INTELLECT SYSTEM

Considering the subsystems of the intellect is an interesting experience, for there are many issues involved, just as in the building of any large software system. As the Intellect as a system takes on shape and substance, it cannot be made too complicated because the functions themselves are already very large and complicated.

The question under consideration is this: Which functional attribute comes first in the mind of an autonomous system constellation: the abstraction (abstract knowledge), or the experiential (hands-on validation of the abstract, or simply direct experience)?

For the purpose of simplifying a complex process and enabling the requirements and design phases, we start with the abstraction; it is, unfortunately for most human beings, the main source of information, mistaken most often for knowledge.

The architecture of the Intellect system is composed of the Noumenon subsystem, the Phenomenon subsystem, the Abstract subsystem, the Experience subsystem, and the Knowledge subsystem.

5.4.1 The Abstract Subsystem

The Abstract subsystem records, files, and processes for use all information acquired from secondary sources. Arthur Schopenhauer is adamant[11] on this point. He is skeptical about the validity and absolute truth of material read in books and newspapers, and received in the classrooms and lectures. All of the information received through secondary sources is open to question. Theater, motion pictures, the Internet, radio, and television today provide abstract data and abstract knowledge. The abstract knowledge provided by secondary sources may be complete, valid, and correct, but the recipient of such knowledge can never be certain. The databases storing abstract knowledge must be validated by physical experience as to whether they are true or not. An individual who has no other knowledge than abstract information can never be certain of the validity of the data until proven by experience.

The autonomous system will be able on its own to interface to online repositories and databases and download any information it needs to do its job. It will also be able to acquire information through other venues, such as viewing, listening, and so on.

5.4.2 The Experience Subsystem

The Experience subsystem stores, files, and processes the knowledge acquired through physical experience. Where the abstract information will not do much to aid the survival of a species, knowledge based on experience is sufficient for a being to survive.

5.4.3 The Knowledge Subsystem

The Knowledge subsystem processes the abstract information and knowledge gained through experience into real and practical knowledge. It processes (evaluates, categorizes, prioritizes, integrates, synthesizes, and stores) the data and applies them in the sum of knowledge needed by the autonomous system to perform its mission accurately and efficiently.

5.5 THE EXTERNAL INTERFACES OF THE INTELLECT SYSTEM

The major interfaces of the Intellect system are the Phenomenon and Noumenon networks. Received through the Phenomenon network are the Intellect-specified data sets provided in one or more data streams or through monads from the external sensors. The external sensors are located on or beyond the outer surface of the body or shell of the autonomous system. These sensors provide the data to the Intellect system as defined by the Sensory system. The data sets it receives are only those which are useful by the Intellect system in raw form or which it can process directly. The external inputs it can use are shapes, masses, motions, and temperatures, among many others.

The other interface, the Noumenon network, operates in the human language selected for internal thinking and communicating among the systems of the constellation.[12] It is through this language that the systems of the constellation engage in monologues, dialogues, and conferences regarding their databases, the validity of their sensory information, and putting substance to the objects under consideration.

CHAPTER 6

The Architecture of the Presentation System

This chapter describes the functional architecture and operation of the Presentation system. The idea and concept for its architecture are derived from the referenced works of Arthur Schopenhauer, as well as those of Immanuel Kant.

The role of the Presentation system is that of the "theater of the mind." The primary functional attribute is the presentation of all sensory data, as well as the sum of all relevant knowledge, to the other systems of the constellation. The Presentation system presents and prepares full Sensory and Thought system data for viewing as a medium for discussion and for contemplation of potential decisions and their consequences. The Presentation, on a continuous basis, takes the preprocessed data from the other systems and formats them into viewable presentations. If the data arrive unprocessed or have been preprocessed only partially, then the Presentation system completes the formatting. It has an endless data stream and endless subject presentation. It is capable of multiple instant playbacks from even the earliest sensory impressions, understandings, and intellectual information, such as knowledge and experience. It is also capable of instantly projecting multiple possible future endings to a scenario or problem, be they pleasant, unpleasant, frightful, painful, and the like, and performs risk analysis based on

The Autonomous System: A Foundational Synthesis of the Sciences of the Mind,
First Edition. Szabolcs Michael de Gyurky and Mark A. Tarbell.
© 2014 John Wiley & Sons, Inc. Published 2014 by John Wiley & Sons, Inc.

input from the Understanding system and recommends a conclusion based on input from the Decision system.

The Presentation system presents audio, visual, and sensory data in real time, and replays and projects future events as real, as though they had already occurred.

This chapter describes at a Level II the architecture and operation of the subsystems of the Presentation system: the Viewing subsystem, the Projection subsystem, the Experience subsystem, the Analysis subsystem, the Recall subsystem, and the Contemplation subsystem.

The external and internal interfaces are also provided in sufficient detail for the development of the autonomous system in keeping with strict and sound engineering practices.

6.1 THE PRESENTATION SYSTEM

In its fundamental aspect, the Presentation system functions as a multimedia theater. In the human mind, its size, functional scope, and processing capacity are almost entirely dependent on the education of the individual. The size of the processor—the human brain in terms of Hegel's quantum—is almost limitless. The human mind is equally immense; in quantum terms, the mind is a universe unto itself. Therefore, it is an individual's responsibility to expand his or her mind through learning complex systems in the categories required for survival as well as for living a civilized life as a citizen of a community. Thus, the mind is like the visible universe on a clear night: In this universe, an individual can build a world of systems, or let it lay empty and underdeveloped.

The applied education is learning through instruction and formal presentation, reading, and experience. The pedagogic part is learning through logic. Logic is a metaphysical science, a science of the spirit, a mental science that is developed only through thinking (e.g., thought experiments).

The development of the world of the human mind is coupled to the degree to which an individual desires to understand the visible world around himself, as well as the invisible world of the inner self.

The word "presentation" is very broad in meaning. In general usage, it is used to mean imagination. In German, however, it means not only imagination, but also presentation in an all-media sense: imaging, sound, taste, form, mass, substance, density, motion, color, temperature, and so on. Therefore, it is a real-time physical presentation, as well as an internal viewing, that is, *Anschauung*. Kant goes so far as to say that the Presentation is in fact the connection among laws, causation, life, and dreams. Therefore, it is not sensual (i.e., from the physical senses), but intellectual, via understanding and recognition *a priori*.[1] In design terms, this connection then is the focal point for the Will, the Reason, the Intellect, and the rest of the systems of the constellation of the mind. When it is in the contemplative mode, viewing is a fantasy or meditation, like the process of using mathematics to solve problems in the head.

Presentation includes all the information acquired through the physical senses as well as the information that is gathered through the metaphysical senses, such as what might be called presentiment or premonition. This is not only in the negative sense, but also in the positive sense. In a very small percentage of the population, this *a priori* conclusion, followed by a decision, is usually attributed to what is considered by the great thinkers as Genius. Hegel for one postulates such metaphysics as "pure speculative philosophy," which is a new way of defining knowledge, that is, *science is knowledge*.

For someone contemplating the pure speculative philosophy of say, Being (*Sein*), it is a delightfully challenging task of study. Moreover, for the computer scientist of the 21st century, as a design issue, it is quite suited for definition, design, and implementation. Testing this system as a whole or as subsystems is much more of a problem than ordinary applications or systems software. Even if many of the difficult issues (e.g., "negation of the negation"[2]) are not of urgent concern to the design architect or team,[3] they must be conversant intimately in classical philosophy, and ideally also in the languages in which they were written. Cognitive philosophy, as a baseline concept for the architecture of the autonomous system, makes the German language and its prior dialects invaluable to the software architect.

The particular human language used in the Thought system (the Nexus Cogitationis and the Noumenon) will play a critical role in the autonomous system's ability to think, learn, decide, and to communicate internally among its systems and externally to man. Thus, a human language rich in vocabulary and grammar is absolutely necessary.[4]

6.2 THE PRESENTATION AS A SYSTEM

The Presentation is a system because of its immense size in operational processing and complexity of functions. It receives input from the external Phenomenon network in real time and presents the input to the other systems of the constellation as it is received. The input is then viewed by the other systems and commented on in the common human language used throughout, until an adequate object is assembled,[5] and then it is retained as an open, human-like data store, where it is enhanced and enlarged and used as needed by the system constellation. This is an ongoing, unending process. Some of the data are abstract, some experiential. These are two separated domains, and the constellation of the mind handles these as valid, each in its own right, until one or the other category is validated as knowledge.

The determination of exactly when the mind is confident that it has real, practical knowledge or simply abstract or experiential knowledge is difficult to know. In human beings, it is as well hidden as the survival instinct presents itself in other species. In human beings, though, it is almost always camouflaged, because humans have a greater capacity to deceive.

6.3 THE SUBSYSTEMS OF THE PRESENTATION

The architecture of the Presentation system is based firmly on the work of Arthur Schopenhauer. The Presentation is indispensable to the human thought process and therefore to the autonomous system's thought process as well. It is the system that in a multimedia format brings images from the world of the Phenomenon to the mind and presents to the other systems in the constellation images, sounds, smells, objects, motion, textures, and so on in a composite multidimensional format in time and space.

The Phenomenon data is physical and is viewed by all other systems of the constellation, which through their impressions and interpretations gives birth to what we call the Idea. As seen from the architecture of the constellation as a whole, each system receives the raw, human-like Phenomenon data also. The other systems act not only as functioning systems, but also as filters of the Phenomenon data. The systems then take the Phenomenon data and process these with their own parameters and translate them into the Noumenon format in human language.

An example would be the image of a tree in the Presentation. As the presentation of the object is being viewed by the systems of the constellation, the Intellect system will identify the object as a tree, the Understanding system as a pine tree, and so on. Identifying a pine tree to the Presentation system and the constellation is done in human language.

In addition to this Phenomenon data, there are the nonphysical or "beyond physical" data. This happens when human beings sleep or are meditative, and shut out all external sensory activity. It is an activity we know very well. It occurs in dreaming and is best described as a type of background processing. These data are what Kant, Hegel, and Schopenhauer called metaphysical or spirit-generated data. These are also transmitted into the Presentation for viewing by all of the systems in the constellation, but without the input from the physical world of the Phenomenon.

This subject is called metaphysical. Having recognized its existence, Kant, Hegel, and Schopenhauer had great difficulties in their efforts to research it, analyze it, and describe it. The roots of their difficulties in presenting it to the academics of their time was that the world even of their day wanted only the physical, empirical sciences, and not the intangible, metaphysical sciences. Nevertheless, we in the software world deal more in intuitive thinking than the other sciences because we deal in languages and in processing architectures. We have taken some of the terms used by Kant, Hegel, and Schopenhauer, and for software engineering purposes, named them subsystems. The effective integration of the subsystems in the Presentation is dependent on the power of the imagination, or *Einbildungskraft*, of the subject as in a human being, and in this instance, as in the autonomous system.

6.3.1 The Viewing Subsystem

The Viewing subsystem processes the data from the Phenomenon and prepares it in time and space for presentation to the other systems of the mind of the autonomous system. It receives through the Thought system, that is, Noumenon, input from the other systems of the constellation, and then includes the added data into the viewing. This process is done spontaneously and simultaneously with dynamic, not sequential, logic.

6.3.2 The Projection Subsystem

The Projection subsystem receives monads through the Noumenon, directly from the systems of the constellation, concerning objects, things, odors, sounds, and forms that the system in question, say the Will or the Reason, wishes to discuss and elaborate on. Take as an example an object like a hand grenade, which the Will system wants to physically pick up, but does not know what it is. So the Intellect system adds to the object being viewed, "That is a hand grenade; it is dangerous to our existence." The Understanding system provides the Form of All Possibilities and adds, "If we pick it up, it could be useful; but if it is booby-trapped, it will destroy us."

6.3.3 The Experience Subsystem

The Experience subsystem provides to the Intellect system's Knowledge subsystem a synthesis of the abstract data it has from lectures and field manuals on the object in question and the experience factor it contains from observation. It counsels the Will and the Reason systems not to take a chance, for example, and to leave the object alone. (The first author has witnessed tragedies resulting from the failure of this scenario during the war in Vietnam.)

6.3.4 The Analysis Subsystem

The Analysis subsystem evaluates the ongoing events and decisions from all of the systems contributing to the Presentation, and prepares databases for instant recall. These analysis files and databases are then shared with the pertinent systems in the constellation for recall and further reference for application. The process is ongoing, but it is a prerequisite of a healthy, advanced, and well-organized human mind to carry out these decisions. Inadequately developed minds are inferior thought systems due to laziness on part of the learner, says Schopenhauer, and are not capable of processing and using this kind of data and information.

6.3.5 The Recall Subsystem

The Recall subsystem is a wide-spectrum subsystem. It is in part a normal, human-like recall on thought searching at moderate speeds and rates. However, as the software architect must address the design for Genius, it is also an instant recall at a glance providing the correct answer to an *a priori* query or situation. In humans, this is rarely possible, but when present, indicates true genius. In case of the autonomous system, it will be more the rule than the exception.

6.3.6 The Contemplation Subsystem

The Contemplation subsystem is the locus of the internal processing and analysis of data. This subsystem is the place where internal memory sources solve problems, either consciously or without awareness of doing so. It is where mathematical problems are worked and solved; this is where poetry and music are written, and great works of art are developed, like the statues of Michelangelo and the oils of da Vinci, Picasso, and Reuben. The contemplation subsystem in humans is a mysterious, metaphysical place where the creative Genius resides. How we duplicate this in an autonomous machine is a complicated question; however, very few human beings have a well-developed version of this subsystem. It must be done because we are searching for the truth, *Objective Truth*.

CHAPTER 7

The Architecture of the Understanding System

This chapter describes the functional architecture and operation of the Understanding, or *Verstand* in German. The idea and concept for its architecture are derived and inferred from the seminal works of Kant, Hegel, and Schopenhauer, and from the software development experience of the authors.

The role of the Understanding is that of "executive officer" of the autonomous system. The primary functional attribute is to continuously compile and present decision items for action in logically formatted packages. The decision item packages contain all relevant items from the other systems and are action-ready.

This chapter describes at a Level II the architecture and operation of its subsystems: the Form of All Appearances subsystem, the Form of All Possibilities subsystem, and the Understanding Preparation subsystem.

The external and internal interfaces are provided in sufficient detail for the development of the autonomous system in keeping with strict and sound software development practices.

The Understanding has the attribute and capability of recognizing and identifying a specific phenomenon, object, or product as a unique thing, and also as part of an analytical whole. It is also capable of identifying and specifying the origins or causes of the thing, object, or

The Autonomous System: A Foundational Synthesis of the Sciences of the Mind,
First Edition. Szabolcs Michael de Gyurky and Mark A. Tarbell.
© 2014 John Wiley & Sons, Inc. Published 2014 by John Wiley & Sons, Inc.

product. These two attributes and processes—*the form of all appearances* and *the form of all possibilities*—produce a third capability in the human mind called *understanding*. It is equally important to note that an impaired or defective understanding in a human being was referred to by Schopenhauer as the *Stumpfkopf*.[1]

> *Wisdom and Genius, these two peaks of the Parnassus of human recognition, are not rooted in the abstract and discursive, but in the faculty to view and comprehend. Wisdom is something intuitive, not abstraction. Wisdom is not composed of rules and thoughts which were acquired by personal research or the research of others which one carries as knowledge around in one's head; but a whole approach, how the entire world is represented in one's mind. This so highly different, that through this, the world the wise man lives in is a world different from the fool's, and the Genius sees a world different from that of the* Stumpfkopf *("dull head"). That the works of the Genius immeasurably surpass the works of all others is only the result of the fact that the world which the Genius sees, and from which his assertions are taken, is so much clearer, and the resulting works undergo a much deeper, detailed, and careful preparation than the works of all other types of minds, which naturally contain the same items, but is like a Chinese picture without the shadows and the perspectives when compared to an oil painting.*

Schopenhauer's *Stumpfkopf* is a self-imposed state or condition of the mind that results when a human being refuses to push him- or herself to intellectual achievement and continuous study with the objective of broadening his or her mind.

In this, we are dealing with an aspect of the human mind that is at once natural, physical, and metaphysical. This metaphysics is no longer the physics of the science of experience, but that which transcends it in so far as it is specified by accepted laws.[2] This definition of metaphysics and its use and application in our everyday work of speculative contemplation of the autonomous system's architecture should make it more acceptable as a tool in 21st-century computer science.

We use Immanuel Kant's work as the primary driver because being much more than mere abstract knowledge, it is his *Kritik der reinen Vernunft* that presents itself for all practical purposes as the functional design of thought.

7.1 THE UNDERSTANDING AS A SYSTEM

The Understanding is a system because it is too large and complex to be a subsystem. In the process of transitioning from the automaton or robot to an autonomous system, we are limited by language and space. As a system, the Understanding produces understanding as a product apart from knowledge, regardless of how extensive and well developed that knowledge may be.

It has three major subsystems, each of enormous complexity:

- The Form of All Appearances subsystem
- The Form of All Possibilities subsystem
- The Understanding Preparation subsystem.

The Understanding is thus the synthesis of the product of all appearances and all possibilities. In addition to these subsystems, there are the two subsystems common to all of the systems in the constellation—the Phenomenon and the Noumenon—through which each system of the constellation receives and sends data, respectively.

Because of the problems inherent in languages, knowledge alone is never sufficient to produce any kind of product. "Understanding" as a term means that one reflects on a situation, a thing, an event, or condition, and considers all of the possibilities the thing represents, beneficial or harmful, desirable or undesirable, which can result from a decision made by the mind, which is the constellation collectively.

Due to the number and frequency of catastrophic examples experienced by the authors of seeing knowledge mistaken for understanding, it became a point of interest and focus, directly resulting in the creation of the Design Hub concept as a method of reducing the risk of failure by as much as 99%.[3]

In a decision process, the above-average, well-developed mind will look first at the appearances of a thing, object, condition, state, or activity, and then at all the possibilities presenting themselves, both collectively and individually, drawing on the Intellect system's Knowledge subsystem, receiving all asked-for updates in the process. The Decision system arbitrates between these two systems using the Presentation system to display to the entire constellation all available data in every possible context via the process of objective viewing. In appropriate moments or under the appropriate circumstances, the

Reason system may be asked for the axioms, rules, and laws governing several of the decisions that may be under consideration. The issue may be a course of action demanded by the Will system, but the ethics under natural or moral law may dictate otherwise. Hence, the decision may be amended or modified, or an entirely different decision made.

7.1.1 Illustration of Understanding Preparation

We consider a simple, brutal, but all-too-human example to illustrate our point. Events such as this clear-cut example happen at all levels, from the individual to the national, some even with global impact.

Kruger National Park, South Africa—This noteworthy event begins when a convoy of cars, filled with tourists and traveling through Kruger National Park in South Africa, comes upon a pride of lions feeding on a kill. The convoy stops to enable the tourists to observe, photograph, and film this scene in the wild. In order to film the feeding lions at close range, one of the men decides to exit his vehicle, leaving his family behind to watch. He is filmed from the other vehicles as he gets out, closes the door, and with camera in hand approaches the lions feeding under a tree. At a distance of a few feet he starts taking photographs of a large lion feeding. The lion suddenly looks up, snarls, and swats the photographer in the head. It then attacks the prone man in full sight of the tourists, kills him, and eats him, while the people in the convoy vehicles film the event, capturing it for the evening news.

Now, in the context of the Understanding system, we analyze this event as a functional process.

The Form of All Appearances
- The scene presents a pride of lions in the wild, feeding on a kill.
- The lions are predators/carnivores, which obviously eat meat to survive.
- The lions are hungry and each gets a share depending on its place in the hierarchy of the pride and the amount of meat available.
- It is clear that at this time of day, the zebra are not enough for them, and they will need to hunt again.

The Form of All Possibilities

- The lions are tame lions, trained by the Kruger National Park rangers and game wardens to entertain the tourists and to increase the number of tourists visiting the park each year.

- The lions are wild lions, but are accustomed to seeing tourists and therefore have no interest in them.

- The lions prefer the flesh of indigenous animals and not tourists because tourist flesh tastes foreign to them.

- It is a common enough event that a person should leave his vehicle, so the lions will ignore him and continue to eat.

- The lions will think that this tourist wants to take away their meal for himself.

- The lions will resent the intrusion and chase the tourist away.

- The lions see the tourist as only a source of meat, and will kill him and eat him if they are hungry.

A functional Understanding system will register to the observers (i.e., other systems in the constellation) that based on an implicit risk-to-benefit analysis of obtaining good photographs versus being maimed or killed, it is best to remain in the vehicle and not to approach the pride of lions feeding, as it is not possible without prior experience to accurately assign realistic probabilities to each of the Possibilities, so it is not possible to ascertain the true nature (wild/tame) or intentions of the lions, and thus the probable outcome of any encounter remains indeterminable.

It is the esoteric lesson of Kantian philosophy that the Understanding may not overshadow the Experience (which we have placed for software engineering purposes into the Intellect system); otherwise, the process of recognition becomes theoretical (abstract) as opposed to practical (based on real knowledge). Thus, in the process of recognition, experience is the dominant factor. It is a part of the Intellect system, where it is the most valuable if the theoretical knowledge is validated through hands-on experience.

7.2 THE EXTERNAL INTERFACES OF THE UNDERSTANDING

The Understanding system interfaces to the external world through the Phenomenon, and to the internal world of the constellation (and thus with all other systems) through the Noumenon in human language. It must be kept in mind that the Viewing of the objects assembled and displayed on the Presentation system is not limited to the initiating process of viewing, but also results from tasting, smelling, feeling, touching, and understanding. This is a dynamic world of processing, sorting, storing, linking, and retrieval, in itself requiring what is called *Denkkraft*, the power to process thought. In modern terms, the input to the constellation is not only from reading and presentation, but also from validation through hands-on experience. The input comes from the Internet, television, motion pictures, radio, books, and all other media. To the weak and underdeveloped mind, this can have disastrous consequences. Thus, the Understanding system is very important to survival and well-being in a thinking, autonomous system.

7.2.1 The Form of All Appearances Subsystem

The architecture of the Understanding system is essentially made up of three basic subsystems. We begin with a discussion of the Form of All Appearances subsystem. The simplest way to start describing the internals of this subsystem is to begin with the listing of the categories of Aristotle.[4] It is not a difficult process; after all, it is the place where dynamic logic started for Hegel in his younger years.

The following categories are not composites, but discrete:

- Substance
- Quantity
- Quality
- Relation
- Place
- Time
- Position
- State
- Action
- Affection.

Aristotlean example:[5]

"To sketch my meaning roughly, examples:
*Of **substance** are 'man' or 'horse.'*
*Of **quantity** such terms as 'two cubits long' or 'three cubits long.'*

*Of **quality** such attributes as 'white' grammatical.*
*Of the category of **relations** fall 'double,' 'half,' 'greater.'*
*Under **place**, as 'in the market place,' 'in the lyceum.'*
*Under **time** fall 'yesterday,' today,' 'last year.'*
*Under **position** fall 'lying,' 'sitting.'*
*Under **state** fall 'shod,' 'armed.'*
*Under **action** fall 'to cauterize,' 'to lance.'*
*Under **affection** fall 'to be lanced,' 'to be cauterized.'"*

The categories are very important components of the autonomous system's ability to think. This fact cannot be overstated because Kant considered the simple categories to be Concepts. Some of the categories of Hegel and the others will be covered as the design progresses; however, it will be necessary for the design team and for the reader to add categories in the modern technical context and to define them well in order for them to be useful. Still, it is of great importance to understand the entire structure, including the reasons and their originators from the time of classical Athens to be able to relate them to the present and take them into the future.

7.2.2 The Form of All Possibilities Subsystem

The Form of All Possibilities subsystem receives from the Form of All Appearances subsystem the viewed object, whole or in parts. The Understanding System projects the object or parts of the object to the Presentation system for viewing and discussion by the other systems in the constellation. Then, the object is substantiated (given substance) by receiving all available Noumenon data from the Will system, the Intellect system, the Reason System, and so on, until there is objective reality, that is, arrival at pure understanding or *Begriffe des reinen Verstandes*. Arrival at the state of pure understanding is only possible with well-developed human minds. However, the architecture of the autonomous system will make it an operational processing reality.

This may be an appropriate place to describe briefly the sequence of the linkage of the arrival of "all pure Concepts of the Understanding."

The logical functions of the Understanding are as follows:

The Quality of the Decision/Verdict

- General decisions
- Particular decisions
- Singular or individual decisions.

Quality

- Agreement
- Disagreement
- Endless.

Relations (linkage of parts or wholes)

- Categorical
- Hypothetical
- Disjunctive.

Modality

- Problematic
- Assertive
- Apodictic.

7.2.3 The Understanding Preparation Subsystem

The Understanding Preparation subsystem assembles and processes the form of all appearances and integrates these data with the form of all possibilities. The process will be an estimate of the situation presented to the Decision system in complete form, with a number of likely scenarios of both positive and negative consequence. These data are projected onto the Presentation system for viewing and consideration by the other systems of the constellation.

CHAPTER 8

The Architecture of the Sensory System

This chapter describes the functional architecture and operation of the Sensory system. The idea and concept for its architecture are based on the works of Kant, Hegel, Schopenhauer referenced in this volume and validated by the experiences gathered by the authors while participating in major spaceflight projects.

The role of the Sensory system is that of environmental awareness, both active and passive. Its primary functional attribute is to monitor all internal states, as well as the environment external to the autonomous system. It is the repository of all mechanical and software systems' standards and limits, with the purpose of ensuring the health of the autonomous system.

This chapter describes at a Level II the architecture and operation of its subsystems: the Autonomous System State subsystem, the Propulsion, Motion, and Manipulation subsystem, and the Standards and Limits subsystem.

The external and internal interfaces are provided in sufficient detail for the development of the autonomous system in keeping with strict software engineering practices.

8.1 THE SENSORY SYSTEM

One of the main triggers for considering sensing as a system occurred during the interesting times the first author experienced as team chief

The Autonomous System: A Foundational Synthesis of the Sciences of the Mind,
First Edition. Szabolcs Michael de Gyurky and Mark A. Tarbell.
© 2014 John Wiley & Sons, Inc. Published 2014 by John Wiley & Sons, Inc.

of the Voyager project general science data team in 1979. During the exciting work we performed, as the spacecraft approached the planet Jupiter, a certain recently published book became of interest. It was titled, *Kant: The Three Critiques*, and was published by Kröner Verlag in Stuttgart. There was a reference in this book by Herr Professor Raymund Schmidt[1] to one of Immanuel Kant's Latin dissertations on sensing: "*De Mundi Sensibilis Atque Intelligibilis Forma et Principiis: Dissertatio*" (Dissertation on the Form and Principles of the Sensible and the Intelligible World). This dissertation connected to a sequence of insights into our daily work in the preparation of Voyager's Experiment Data Records (EDRs) and Supplementary Experiment Data Records (SEDRs). We prepared these records from the data stream we received from the two Voyager spacecraft through our Deep Space Network. These records were processed on our IBM 360/70 computers and printed out as hardcopy on our 14 large line printers and also put onto magnetic tape. These were provided to the users directly, and were also transmitted remotely to those users unable to be physically present for the encounter with Jupiter. The science data originated from the sensors aboard these two spacecraft. These sensors are instruments that had been designed by the principal investigators (PIs) of the project, and provided the science and engineering data necessary for completion of their experiments. The results of the experiments in turn were published in numerous scientific publications.

This was exciting work; we were learning new information from the world around us. More importantly, we were learning about the advanced technology in the science and engineering of sensors as things which were to be the mechanical replications of human sensory attributes.

To a software architect, the Voyager spacecraft, with its onboard computer, its numerous sensors, as well as the ground organization flying and commanding it represented an analogous model of remote sensing, data processing, and packaging for use. Everything Kant was saying about how human beings sense, think, perceive, contemplate, and decide was accomplished within the framework of a super-sophisticated "biological computer system."

The world around us and within us "exists" for us because it is an array of objects we perceive through our senses (sight, touch, taste, hearing, and smell). It was an interesting insight that the Phenomenon data were prepared by us on the Voyager team regarding the world around the spacecraft in Experiment Data Records (the "phenomena" around the spacecraft), and the data regarding the state of the spacecraft itself (the "phenomena" inside the spacecraft), also in the form of Experiment Data Records. This hypothesis was to prove itself correct in the years after the Jupiter encounters. However, there was still much that had to happen and much to be learned through observation and experience until the Ocean Topographic Explorer (TOPEX-Poseidon) spacecraft project came along in 1989.

The Sensory system is responsible for the acquisition, processing, linking, coupling, formatting, and delivery of all environmental data to the constellation of the mind of the autonomous system, that is, to the systems responsible for all the cognitive functions of the autonomous system. The world from which it receives input, the Phenomenon, is huge in size and is set in time and space.

The Sensory is a system because of the complexity of the design challenges it poses. For our design purposes, the autonomous system is the pilot and crew of an interplanetary spacecraft, and therefore designed to operate and exist in deep space, so the sensory requirements are more complex than ours since we live in an atmosphere-covered planet.

8.2 THE ARCHITECTURE OF THE SENSORY SYSTEM

The architecture of the sensory system is composed necessarily of hardware and software. The sensory and instrumentation equivalent of a spacecraft is the hardware, which provides the data to the Sensory system for processing and to the rest of the systems of the constellation of the mind for use as an operational necessity. Thus, the major subsystem is necessarily the Phenomenon subsystem; the lesser subsystems are the Noumenon subsystem, the Propulsion, Motion, and Manipulation subsystem, the Standards and Limits subsystem, and the Autonomous System State subsystem.

The Level I external interfaces of the Sensory system are the sensors themselves. The sensors provide the data for the Phenomenon subsystem to process and build a continuous image of the physical world around the autonomous system. These data are provided by the Phenomenon network. After processing the data, the Sensory system converts the data into human language and projects them onto the Presentation system for viewing and discussion. In a way, the Phenomenon subsystem presents the equivalent of Voyager's EDRs and SEDRs in real time to the Presentation system as an ongoing operation. This process, as an ongoing rational phenomenon, would be unimaginable were it not for Hegel's view of the quantum and his concept of the mathematics involved.

8.3 THE PHENOMENON SUBSYSTEM

The English word "phenomenon" comes from the Greek φαινόμενον or *phainomenon*, meaning a thing appearing to the view (of the physical senses).

The external data are received in an unending stream of data packets of impressions. This process is the "oneness of the endless and unending."[2]

8.3.1 The External Sensory Program Set

The External Sensory program set is composed of the sensors observing the external environment of the autonomous system.

This program set has a task-oriented array of sensor programs. In our case, sensory programs that are appropriate for space exploration would include:

- Size detection and the continuation of the moment of discretion
- Mass detection and its unending and unlimited quantum (quality and mathematics), including the physical and "spiritual" quanta (matter without mass), as in Hegel's *Phänomenologie des Geistes*.
- Form detection in all presentations
- Motion detection: Newton's thoughts on motion and acceleration in time and space
- Photonic detection: frequency, energy, quantity, color distribution, and temperature
- Radioactivity detection
- Charged particle detection
- Plasma detection.

8.3.2 The Internal Sensory Program Set

The Internal Sensory program set is composed of the sensors monitoring the performance of the components of the hardware (electromechanical) bus.

The internal sensor programs will have to monitor and process internal sensor input related to:

- Joint Operation
- Standards and Limits
- Parts:
  - Mechanical
  - Electrical
  - Optical
  - Motorized
- Temperatures
- Radiation Exposure Levels
- Wear, Fitness, and Age
- Energy:
  - Systemic Voltage Levels
  - Systemic Storage Levels
  - Sources:
    - Solar Radiation
    - Radio Thermal Generator
    - Gasses for Ion Propulsion, Solar Sails, and so on
  - Systemic Requirements.

It is not our intention to get into the business of sensor design. However, there will be many stated, implied, and derived requirements for the autonomous system's sensors,[3] as well as materials. The Voyager I spacecraft will pass within 1.6 light-years of the star Gliese 445 in some 40,000 earth years. Voyager II will be make its closest approach (4.3 light-years) to the star Sirius in about 296,000 earth years. Certainly, with the current state of the art in technology and science, it would be an unachievable goal to expect such longevity from the hardware systems sent on such journeys unless they were to incorporate the means of self-repair and self-renewal, not only of hardware but in the case of an autonomous system, of psyche as well.[4] These two extreme reference points will make the survival of the computers as well as the sensors very important design requirements. With the advances recently made in areas such as optical, biological, and quantum computing, it may well be that the computers on board will be fabricated from materials that are not so influenced by charged particle fields or stray electromagnetic fluxes. The external sensors in any case will need to be of the most durable materials available, able to be replicated and to withstand the conditions of deep space for as long as possible. Internally, the sensors monitoring the health and state of the system are easier to protect from elements like electromagnetic pulses and cosmic rays, but they, too, will succumb eventually to the accumulated effects sustained radiation has on materials.

8.3.3 The Sensory Data Processing Program Set

The Sensory Data Processing program set prepares the Sensory Phenomenon Data Records (external sensing) and the Engineering Phenomenon Data Records (internal sensing). These data records are processed in physical time, when the system is active.

When the autonomous system is in an inactive or safehold mode of many years, as it would be during extended cruise periods, it is in a human-like sleep state and in contemplative time. When the system is shut down for maintenance or rest, it will be in a dreamlike state and will use its mind—the systems of the constellation—to think and to solve problems not based on physical experience.[5]

The Sensory system data are projected in an ongoing, never-ceasing stream to the Presentation system in a real-time all-media (imaging, sound, color, temperature, etc.) holographic viewing (*Anschauung*) format in time and space. This real-time situation display is then enhanced and modified by all new data available from the systems of the constellation. Awake or asleep, each autonomous system independently from the others thinks and does contemplative replays ("dreams"), and communicates in human language through the Noumenon in the form of dialogues, monologues, broadcasts, and conferences in the interrogative, dative, ablative, and imperative modes, in both decision-oriented and contemplative states.

The Noumenon has an internal language interface to the Thought system. The Noumenon (νοούμενον, from the Greek νοεῖν, *noien*; literally, "something conceived") is inextricably integrated into the structure of the Thought system; the two are inseparable. Through this interface, it provides the composite sensory data acquired through the external and internal sensing to the other systems in the constellation. The object and its parts and attributes are named, labeled, and discussed in the internal human language of the autonomous system.

8.4 A HISTORICAL PERSPECTIVE ON LANGUAGES

In the *Critique of Pure Reason* (*Kritik der reinen Vernunft*), Immanuel Kant used the Greek word νοούμενον for "concept and thought" to express his idea of the architectural object and the associated process of how human beings think.

Recall that at the time Kant, Hegel, and Schopenhauer were writing, the process of transitioning to the use of national languages for science and engineering had begun. This presented a twofold problem. First, none of the national languages had an adequate vocabulary or grammar to fully express complex science and engineering concepts or ideas, much less design or implementation issues that were testable. Second, most of the great minds of the period did not speak national languages other than their own and Latin, Greek, and Hebrew. Since great scholars like Renatus Cartesius (aka René Descartes) and Isaac Newton wrote in Latin and Greek, there was no need to learn other languages. The period surrounding the French Revolution was used by nation-states like England, France, Prussia, Italy, and Spain to expand their languages for the use of science and engineering. Some of these languages, like German, were more adaptable; others less so. It required great effort to use Greek and Latin words and concepts and to integrate them into the national languages to permit serious research and design.

From a software architectural point of view, it is appropriate to use the term *noumenon*, which means *to think* or *apprehend*. Since the term is a functional object of intellectual perception, Kant elevated it to *Das Ding an sich*, a thing unto itself, an object of purely intellectual intuition. Thus, we can appreciate how much of a struggle the great researchers had reinventing their national languages to make them suitable for science and engineering. This likewise serves to underscore how complex and vulnerable languages are to misinterpretation.

8.5 THE WORKINGS OF THE NOUMENON

The Internal Sensory projects its acquired sensory data through the Noumenon as a composite object to the Presentation system and tags it with a simple question: *What is this*? The object image may be based on experience or on contemplation, so it may be a reality or a fantasy of the mind. The question is then responded to by the Reason system, the Will system, the Understanding system, the Decision system, and the Intellect system. Each system independently processes the external sensory information it receives from the Phenomenon. When the Sensory system projects its thought fragment—*Logos* or *Gedanken-stücke*[6]—onto the Presentation, the other systems view it and add their own fragments of data. This process in human beings becomes very complicated. It is for this reason that the classical philosophers were fortunate not to have too many social taboos and *Schranke* (gates, obstacles, social limitations) placed in their paths. Science knows no social limitations; if it did, it would no longer be science.

The concept of freedom of thought was limited over time by political powers and the mental limitations of those who wielded those powers. It was not quite as bad during the time of Aristotle, Socrates, and Plato as it is today. Alexander the Great of Macedonia was an open-minded monarch, as was Frederick the Great of Prussia. Most kings, emperors, and societies were not open-minded. This issue is then impacted by the richness and precision of the languages in which humans think, keeping in mind that logic is "pure thought." Languages possessing a precise grammar and a rich vocabulary like Latin are subject to fewer misunderstandings.

Human beings, even the most advanced, with well-developed languages and well-developed minds, have some terrible flaws in perception, communication, and judgment. The Will, being what it is, is not only the metaphysical *prius* within all of us, but in all living things and, according to most of the great thinkers, in the entire visible and invisible universe.

This digression is necessary to put ideas and concepts into perspective, especially into the perspective of existing conditions. It is important to understand that the autonomous system is not just an Idea; it is a true Concept.

We can now understand and appreciate the complexity of the functional design of the Sensory system. It receives the internal systems state data in the form of small fragments of sensory perception—the *Logos* of a jigsaw puzzle—and transmits these to the Presentation system. The internal systems state data are composed of sound, motion, odor, taste, pressure fragments, and so on, plus the preference categories of like and dislike. This represents an opportunity for the identification of the interfaces and/or the design of the links connecting each *Logos* with perhaps countless others.

CHAPTER 9

The Architecture of the Decision System

This chapter describes the functional architecture and operation of the Decision system. The idea and concept for its architecture are based primarily on Immanuel Kant's works. However, much is also owed to Hegel and Schopenhauer, filtered through the experience the authors gained over many years of building large software projects.

The role of the Decision system is that of "chief of staff" of the autonomous system. It uninterruptedly assembles information in need of immediate decision and action. It has a list of priorities for selecting courses of action based on survival and the accomplishment of the mission objectives.

This chapter describes at a Level II the architecture and operation of its subsystems: the Value subsystem, Decision Processing subsystem, and the Arbitration subsystem.

The external and internal interfaces are provided in sufficient detail for the development of the autonomous system in keeping with strict and sound engineering practices.

9.1 THE PROCESS OF DECISION MAKING

This chapter addresses the functional aspects and process of making decisions. It is a synthesis of Immanuel Kant's work in this area, and

The Autonomous System: A Foundational Synthesis of the Sciences of the Mind,
First Edition. Szabolcs Michael de Gyurky and Mark A. Tarbell.
© 2014 John Wiley & Sons, Inc. Published 2014 by John Wiley & Sons, Inc.

to a lesser degree, that of Arthur Schopenhauer and G.W.F. Hegel. Added to this synthesis and newly constructed thesis are observations gained during extended combat operations over a period of three years in the armed forces at the rifle company level and below, and the subsequent addition of the observations[1] on decision-making on spacecraft command and control system projects. Experience and observation underpin the validity of personal participation for the formation of all laws required for understanding. Spacecraft command, control, and communications systems in the form of software architecture, as well as their actual use by very highly qualified human beings, represent a surprisingly well-fitting abstraction of the human processes and functions at the macro (project) level.

On the surface, decision making as an act or event is not an issue often thought about in everyday life, yet the process of making rational decisions in the human element is very important and significant. A wrong decision made by an individual can and often does have tragic consequences. On a group level, such as in an infantry unit in combat, it can have disastrous consequences, even the loss of an entire army. On the level of corporate operations, it can destroy the corporation, with the accompanying loss of jobs and income. Wrong decisions made at the level of the financial markets and banking systems can destroy banks, investments, individual savings, and ruin lives. The devaluation of currencies, such as what happened to the German Reichsmark between 1920 and 1930, can bring with it the destruction of a nation.[2] At the national level, a wrong decision is costly in the loss of money.[3] The subject of decision and judgment is daunting to contemplate and cannot be ignored, as decisions, verdicts, tastes, and preferences are so important both on a personal level as well as collectively. For this reason, great emphasis has been placed on decision making by the U.S. Army of the past.

Modeling the decision process of the cognitive functions of the autonomous system is probably the most complex problem ever presented to a software architect or systems engineer. There is the baseline model presented by Immanuel Kant in his *Kritik der Urteilskraft* (The Critique of Decisions) along with certain works by Hegel and Schopenhauer, where they are used to illuminate and add substance to the model of the process. However, these models are by our own definition mere abstractions, and become practical knowledge only after being validated through hands-on experience.

9.1.1 Validation of the Decision Process

One may validate the decision process through experience by close observation in a laboratory-like, controlled environment. Surprisingly, there is no better an example of this than what was presented by the U.S. Army in its training programs of the 1950s. If there was one particular outstanding and memorable maxim from this era, which still echoes in the minds of the surviving few, it is the loud, urgent order of the tactical instructors to the trainees: "*Make a decision, candidate! Make a decision! Now!*" Teaching the process of making a decision to those selected for leadership roles and positions was paramount in the minds of the U.S. Army training cadre.

In retrospect, the emphasis placed by the U.S. Army on the process of making a decision and all its auxiliary processes (functions, and products or results) was very well founded. As an exemplary demonstration of the process of making a decision, consider the U.S. Army's Leadership Reaction Course[4] in 1960. It was the policy of the 7th U.S. Army to have all its noncommissioned officers (NCOs)[5] attend this course regardless of whether the NCO in question had attended similar academies or not. This rigorous, laboratory-like environment was never duplicated anywhere in the services, so it is important to describe it as a practical exercise in a laboratory.

The initial conditions were dictated by the prospects of a World War III against the Union of Socialist Soviet Republics (USSR). This eventuality made it all but certain that it would be started by the USSR as a surprise attack. If this occurred, it meant that at least initially the United States and its allies would be outnumbered at a minimum ratio of $3:1$ or higher. The mandatory requirement for all individuals participating in the Academy was the ability to make correct decisions on the spot, with virtually no time lag. The reason for the no time lag requirement was that at the squad, platoon, and company level the NCOs were the most likely to be first on the scene of combat with their men, as indeed it often happened in all-out ground combat when many of the company-level officers were either killed or wounded. Only at higher command levels, such as the battalion, regiment, and division, is there some time available for deliberation and decision.

The Leadership Reaction Course was surrounded by a solid ten-foot-high fence and had but one entrance and one exit. Inside the fenced area were some thirty to fifty individually numbered physical puzzles.

Each puzzle required the cooperative effort of nine men to solve, working to assemble the materials piled up and ready for use. Each event was timed at ten minutes for assembling the materials correctly and moving on to the next puzzle. The puzzles were complicated, and composed of relatively heavy items, such as fifty-five-gallon oil drums, chains, ropes, pulleys, perforated steel planking, and tools directly related to the everyday type of work encountered in military operations. No one was permitted an early peek at the puzzles or to take pictures of them; this ensured that no one could plan beforehand how to solve them. Each participating squad was assigned ten puzzles and given a total of one hundred minutes to complete the set for a maximum score of one hundred points, which was a grade of "A." A grade under 70% was a failing grade of "F."

The requirements placed upon the development of leaders at the Leadership Reaction Course constituted a "make or break" part of the curriculum. Failing it would result in failing to graduate. The motivation to pass this part of the program was engineered into the design of the course; that is, it was group scored. This meant that as opposed to earning an individual performance score, each individual in the nine-man unit would receive the score the group earned.

Each team of nine men arrived at the Leadership Reaction Course and was briefed upon entrance by a tactical NCO, usually a sergeant first class E-7. The senior member of the squad was given the number of the puzzles to be solved, and with stopwatch ticking, entered the course and went directly to the first puzzle to begin to try to solve it.

In this case, one squad had a master sergeant as team leader; a private first class was present also. As the team went into the first puzzle, the members naturally looked for instruction from their senior member, the MSGT. Unfortunately, he had no clue what to do. The other members of the team had no ideas either. As the seconds ticked away, the stress of time running out and not getting anywhere mounted; the tactical NCO announced that there were now only six minutes remaining. This increased the stress and confusion in the group. Finally, with only four minutes remaining, the young PFC reluctantly spoke up. After all, he was the most junior member of the group, and no one had asked for his opinion.

The team members abruptly stopped talking and looked at him in surprise. At their urging, the young soldier explained quickly how to solve the problem. It took all of the remaining three minutes to scramble and assemble the parts in the correct order. From here on, the PFC was the designated and *de facto* team leader, and the squad deferred to him on every puzzle. The entire team got the maximum grade of 100%—an "A"—for the test of puzzle-solving, cooperation, and decision making.

This remarkable exercise illustrated why Napoleon Bonaparte, the greatest field commander of his time and one of the greatest in history, coined the maxim: "There is a field marshal's baton in every soldier's knapsack." Almost every one of Napoleon's marshals was a former enlisted soldier.

This, then, is the laboratory-like environment that drew the attention of a well-educated and quick-thinking young individual to the study of military tactical analysis, deliberation, decision, and execution as covered in Immanuel Kant's *Kritik der Urteilkraft*.

The designers of an autonomous system must take careful consideration of how the system, once completed and operational, will decide on issues without human intervention. To the systems architect and project manager, this issue is a modern categorical imperative. Why build a system with flaws identical to those of our own, only to be held in regret later?

For this reason, it bears to keep in mind that this chapter is the transition from the work done so laboriously by Immanuel Kant from his days at the University of Königsberg in the Kingdom of Prussia through to the present day's state of technical preparedness in software development.

For practical reasons, we are treating Immanuel Kant as a principal investigator (PI) for the design of the cognitive functions of the autonomous system. To those involved in the design of the interplanetary space flight projects, the PIs provide their vision of how a mission design should work. The system can be set to any application requiring autonomy; for our application, we have chosen a spacecraft with autonomous functions. With such cognitive abilities, there could be one or more such systems manning the spacecraft on its deep space mission.

9.2 UNDERSTANDING THE DECISION PROCESS

The Decision system is based extensively on Immanuel Kant's great work, *Kritik der Urteilskraft*, first published in 1790,[6] a little prematurely at his own insistence. It was eventually republished because of numerous problems in grammar, wording, and spelling. The third edition referenced here is a reprint with corrections published in 1799 in Berlin. This work is the last of his three great masterpieces in the field of the critique. It addresses itself to the three important cultural domains: science, ethics, and the arts.

This Critique had a distinguished following after it was published. The group of individuals deeply influenced by Kant included Johann Wolfgang von Goethe and Johann Friedrich von Schiller. In this Critique, Kant addresses the arts, of which he considered poetry[7] and mathematics[8] to be the greatest form of correct *a priori* conclusions. A "correct" decision means that the decision has the correct construction of relationships among the systems of the mind on a perception presented for consideration.

A correct conclusion followed by a correct decision simply on the understanding of an object is the "mark of Genius" in Kant's proposition. The construction of relationships *a priori* are based on what he calls *Erkenntnisquellen*, "wells of recognition" or "sources of knowledge," which are the property of the Decision system, and are justly considered the mark of Genius. Goethe and Schiller are truly great literary figures who featured high in the politics of their lifetimes, as well as being individual men of high intellectual standing in their respective professions and in society. These two stand shoulder to shoulder with William Shakespeare, and yet they were not only literary figures, but also psychologists and philosophers in their own right.

It is noteworthy here to recall Napoleon's remark to one of his generals as Goethe entered the conference room at Erfurt. Napoleon did not know Goethe personally but immediately turned to his general and said *"Voilà un homme!"* ("Now there is a man!"). Whatever motivated Bonaparte issue this remark to the author of *Werther* is unknown, but Napoleon was a man who knew people, as he had to, having gone from a young Corsican immigrant to a general unequaled on the battlefields, rising to first consul of the French Republic and then crowning himself emperor of the French. Bonaparte was by any measure gifted with a superior mind and had the attribute of Genius. Napoleon's term for his ability to make an *a priori* decision correctly was *un coup d'œil* ("at a glance of an eye"), which is a superb description of a very complex architectural form and process. This process, which has a complex architecture and includes the function of *Anschauung* or contemplation, viewing in both forms—sensual (as per the physical senses:

seeing, hearing, touching, etc.) and intellectual or spiritual (intuition, sentiment, etc.)[9]—is the function of *Erkenntnis* or "recognition knowledge" and the function of *Urteil* or decision.

Almost all of Napoleon's decisions on the battlefields of Europe were fast and correct; this gave him superiority over his opponents. His only *a priori* decision that was tragically wrong was to return from his exile on the island of Elba, claiming that he had to "save France." No one can save a nation or people except the people themselves. Napoleon wound up on St. Helena after the Battle of Waterloo.[10] St. Helena was a harsh place, whereas the island of Elba had been a great place for exile. As we have said, when heads of state make incorrect decisions, they have tragic consequences to themselves as well as to the people they are leading. Napoleon cost France the lives of some 3 million of her young men.

Certainly, the mere understanding of the decision process and architecture presented by Kant, Hegel, and Schopenhauer is not enough to design the architecture of an autonomous system. By their definition, reading provides only abstract information. For a true understanding of Napoleon as a soldier, leader, and commander-in-chief, one must actually serve on the battlefield as a soldier and officer in order to gain experience. This experience is gained by observation and participation in combat operations and by the witnessing of both mistakes and correct results of costly operations. It is absolutely necessary to have as correct, as true, as real an understanding as possible of the contents of the material used in the discussion of the decision process described by a PI. Immanuel Kant is about as great a mind as one could hope to have for a PI.

9.3 THE DECISION AS A SYSTEM

We have elected to raise the function of the decision process to the status of a system in order to make it easier to deal with in issues of design. The Decision system in particular is very large in scope. The meaning of the German word *Urteilskraft* is broad. *Urteil* means verdict and judgment, and *Kraft* means power and energy, but also ability and capability. In our book, *The Cognitive Dynamics of Computer Science*,[11] an important factor in project management and leadership called "dynamic energy," which comes close to *Urteilskraft*, is introduced. This term refers not only to the mental capacity of the manager to estimate the requirements and work situation, but also the capacity to understand all of the parameters surrounding a project. This includes knowing the solutions to problems that arise, being able to marshal the physical and mental energy required to organize the material and staff, and focusing the work and making the decisions required to "carry through" and ensure through supervision and attention to detail that the task is accomplished.

There is, however, much more to *Urteilskraft* than judgment or verdict. It includes also the development of the concepts of esthetic value and teleological judgments, which in an autonomous system must lead to the development of likes, dislikes, and preferences.

The autonomous system must be human-like in the process of how it functions when in the completed state. Likes and dislikes and ideas of something being attractive and desirable or repulsive and undesirable are a part of the development of the human mind. There is much to be said of these functions, attributes, and processes that would fill many volumes of requirements, design documents, and interface specifications from the functional down to the bit level before implementation can begin.

The idea of *Urteilskraft* is daunting indeed; the totality of the definition is phenomenal in its scope. We use terms like "bad judgment" and "bad decision" in business, politics, and everyday life. At the level of technical design, such as in computer science, the consequences of bad judgment manifest themselves in high cost overruns and even the loss of entire projects. Thus, we approach this functional process as a system with a certain awe and humility.

9.4 THE SUBSYSTEMS OF THE DECISION SYSTEM

The subsystems of the Decision system are:

- The Value subsystem
- The Decision Processing subsystem
- The Arbitration subsystem.

9.4.1 The Value Subsystem

The Value subsystem in this functional design is a constantly refreshed template and database processor. This processor draws its information on demand from the other systems in the constellation, storing it for routine operations, such as contemplation or study, and for emergency applications, such as the "fight or flight" reaction. It organizes values into a formal, ever-changing database. The values are needed for *Anschauung*, including physical and internal viewing. The fields of these categories for software purposes reside in the Knowledge subsystem of the Intellect system. The other important sources are the Reason system and the Understanding (*Verstand*) system.

All of the systems in the constellation are more or less equal in the mind of the autonomous system, as opposed to the biological human being where the Will is almost always dominant. The lower the capacity for processing the data of Knowledge, Understanding, Reason, Presentation, and the Intellect, the closer the biological human is to the basic intelligent categories of the animal world. For the computer scientist of today, it is important to understand that these subsystems are linked together through dynamic logic.

The Categories are indispensable to the making of rational decisions. Categories are, or represent, the general concepts we humans need for understanding a thing, an object, and a causation (*Ding, Objekt, Ursache*). It is the Categories that form the baseline for the development of concepts (*Begriffe*) that are needed to identify (*Anschauung*) and think (*Denken*) about objects perceived or seen in nature and presented through the Phenomenon. The ability and capacity to generate and to apply the ability by the autonomous system is what takes place in the Understanding system (*Verstand*: the form of all appearances and possibilities). All decisions, preferences, and tastes are built on the Categories. Thus, the Categories in the Decision system that are in the verdict (*Urteil*) are exactly that: decisions and judgments. The Categorical Imperative is in effect the postulate of a thing, object, or causality.

For this reason, Kant's *Critique of Pure Reason* should be treated as an essential textbook, to be read and reread by the modern computer scientist, systems architect, systems engineer, and manager-architect, or those wishing to become one. Programmers are not required to be deeply read into these foundations; they need to understand the computer languages they are writing in and must be well versed in the art of translating software design documents written at Levels IV and V (the routine and bit level designs, respectively) into esthetic, robust, extensible, and maintainable code.

The numerous footnotes to the original works that are included in this book are necessary. This is because when the actual functional design and functional requirements work starts, the members of the design team need to understand as clearly as possible the intent and meaning Kant, Hegel, and Schopenhauer had in mind as they prepared the material in their various works. However, because the words used by these scholars are often archaic, it is important to remember that we must implement the system using currently in-use technical English, if that is possible.

9.4.1.1 The Value Categories

The primary categories are presented here in order to provide an initial overview and an understanding of the task at hand. As stated previously, we include the categories from Aristotle, Kant, Hegel, and Schopenhauer. The readers and those who are designers and developers will certainly add many more as their understanding is broadened through need and necessity. Arthur Schopenhauer may not be easy to accept because of the tough position he takes on the learning process and the broadening of the mind: "No need, no higher brain."[12] In this respect, Schopenhauer exercises his right of freedom of expression and speech and thought so wonderfully expressed by the great philosopher Fichte.[13]

- *Preferences* are by definition derived from the Latin *praeferre*, to carry in front, to bear.
- *Usefulness* (or "practicality") is exemplified by the quality of practicability as applied to the decisions the Decision system will offer. It will assess its own potential decisions and assign each a degree of Usefulness and applicability toward the resolution of the current problem the autonomous system is contemplating. It is practical in that it aids the Will system in selecting a right and proper course of action by providing it with weighted decisions. In this sense, it is appropriate to use the German word *Zweckmäßigkeit*, as it describes the meaning completely and with precision.
- *Values* are a set of principles, standards, and qualities deemed worthwhile and desirable for general applications. We enter into the domain of what Hegel calls *Phänomenologie des Geistes*, the "domain of 'spiritual' phenomena." This is the metaphysical science of causation and Being (*Sein*).
- *Happiness* is the pursuit of it, as the final purpose of nature.
- *Freedom* is in this case the freedom of the Will.[14]

- *Aesthetics*, *Geschmacksurteile* ("judgments of taste"), is a very important category in that it carries with it a very large field of definitions and processes. This cannot be swept aside as we do in simple modern English. The process of learning to develop wants and desires starts with an impact on the sensory system. As such, Kant correctly raises aesthetics to the status of the Critique. In fact, the *Kritik der Urteilskraft* began its existence as the *Kritik der Geschmacksurteile*.

The autonomous system is not biological; it is necessarily electromechanical, made of metals, plastics, and crystalline matter. Therefore, we need to examine the processes of tastes and preferences as abstract functions.

9.4.2 The Decision Processing Subsystem

The Decision Processing subsystem is both a process and a functional object. What is important to understand is that we are dealing with a software architectural interpretation of the philosophical description of the process. The Decision system presented here is a master processor for *the entire* constellation. The decision process bases its operation on the recognition requiring an action. This action is not sequential, nor is it hierarchical: it is a constant and dynamic process that covers the development of databases necessary for making a decision.

There are two forms of decisions human beings make: *a priori*[15] decisions, which are almost always wrong, and *a posteriori*[16] decisions, which are correct more often than not. Thus, the Decision system should be taken as a single, large, complex process resulting in either an *a priori* or *a posteriori* decision.[17]

9.4.2.1 The Decision Process

The process of formulating a decision, judgment, or preference starts with an input from the sensory system, which can be physical or speculative in nature. It is important to remember that judgment is an identical linkage between subject and predicate.[18] The input can be from the external sensory system we call the Phenomenon, which provides an impression either from the external environment or of the internal systems' state of the constellation. The Sensory system projects the data in a holographic-like form, displayed onto the Presentation system as either an entire object phenomenon or as a fragment of information for the constellation to be aware of. The presentation is three-dimensional in time and space, with sound, texture, shape, motion, and so on. In a sound and healthy human mind, even if uncultured and undeveloped, the object, event, or fragment is examined and completed according to the best information available. It is presented to the constellation through the Noumenon, the internal communication system, as a thought fragment or a completed thought, in a human language communication.

The logic of the decision-judgment is dynamic and begins in unbroken time with awareness of a perception received from sensory input. It is recognized as it is projected in the imagination of the Presentation system by the formation of a mental picture. This picture is enhanced in moments without a break in the process, and the concept begins to take shape. This concept is desirable or undesirable, attractive or repulsive, dangerous or benign. If found to be desirable or gratifying, a judgment or decision is made purely on the impulse of emotion and sensual want or rejection. This type—the *a priori* judgment—is in most cases *wrong* because it has no empirical evidence to support itself, for either good or bad. In rare instances, the *a priori* decisions made by an individual are consistently correct (i.e., not by chance); this phenomenon is called Genius.

In the rational human being, the decision process begins with the formation of a concept. The object of the concept enters what Kant refers to as the *Quellen der Erfahrung* or "wells of experience." There are many such repositories, databases, or wells. For the purpose of this functional design, we shall call these the *wells of knowledge*, the substance of which resides in the Intellect system.

Recall that only abstract information validated by experience gives real knowledge. In the absence of knowledge, experience alone will be made to suffice. Abstract data or knowledge will not suffice in an autonomous cognitive system any more than it does in a human being, at best being a laboriously long and costly learning experience (e.g., the gaining of experience by "on-the-job" training at great expense).

This is where an object viewed as either a fragment or in its entirety is materially enhanced from the individual's wells of knowledge to assure that the decision made is based on substance, not desire.

9.4.2.2 The Wells of Knowledge

The primary wells of knowledge include repositories containing varying degrees of experience with numerous domains, such as:

- Organization
- Leadership
- Academic qualifications
- Management experience
- Understanding of processes and designs
- Communication: written, verbal, and graphic
- Rules and abstractions
- Cognitive dynamics
- Computer science
- Engineering design
- Philosophy
- Classical and modern languages
- Work estimation
- Architecture
- Software management standards
- Methodologies
- Mathematics
- Pure logic.

The synthesis of the knowledge available in the wells of knowledge is the essence of Kant's *Kritik der reinen Vernunft* (The Critique of Pure Reason).[19] The wells of knowledge are categorized into degrees of knowledge, which can be summarized into more or less discrete levels:

- Novice/student: up to 5 years of working in a field
- Apprentice: up to 10 years working in a field.
- Professional: up to 20 years working in a field
- Senior: up to 30 years working in a field
- Principal: more than 30 years working in a field.

The result of the synthesis of the knowledge and the recognition of the object requiring decision, judgment, or verdict is an *a posteriori* judgment.

The U.S. Army had a saying in the 1950s and 1960s that properly and accurately summed up *a priori* decisions; it was referred to as "going off half-cocked."[20] Familiarity with the half-cock safety feature of the M-1911 Colt .45 caliber service pistol is essential because of the many accidents this "feature" caused. In this vein, it is also understandable why Immanuel Kant set such high value on experience as an absolute necessity for making value judgments, sound verdicts, and rational decisions.

9.4.3 The Arbitration Subsystem

The Arbitration subsystem is the primary interface and umpire for the Understanding, Reason, and Intellect systems in its role of generating axioms, rules, and laws.[21]

To give a clearer understanding of this very important functional process, we must look carefully at the following three simultaneously functional roles:

- The *Understanding system* is the *a priori* lawgiver leading to theoretical recognition for all natural objects impacting the senses.

- The *Reason system* is the *a priori* lawgiver of freedom and its own causality beyond the subject's physical senses leading to an unconditional practical recognition.

- The *Intellect system* provides the foundation of the lawgiving process from its abstraction database, its experience database, and in some cases, from its knowledge database, if there is one (in which abstract data has been validated through personal experience sufficiently to be considered knowledge). This process is dynamic and nonlinear, and is unbounded by time as a completed task, flowing onto the Presentation and always either physically or mentally evaluated, updated, and formalized as a axiom, law, or rule. The Intellect system is the processor of likes and dislikes, of what is desirable or undesirable, attractive or unattractive, useful or not useful. It builds tastes and preferences constantly.

In this role, the Arbitration subsystem of the Decision (not isolated, but considered together with the systems of the constellation) is referred to by Kant in German as the *Gemüt* or primary mind. The *Gemüt* is an important term, often misunderstood. It includes the Will, the Thought, the Understanding, the Sensory, the Reason, the Presentation, and the Intellect. In human beings, when all systems of the mind are in harmony without conflicts (e.g., between the desires of the Will system and the moral or ethical stance of the Reason system), then the systems are referred to as being *Gemütlich*.

9.5 THE INTERFACES OF THE DECISION SYSTEM

The Level I external interfaces of the Decision system are the same as for all of the individual systems of the constellation. There are fundamentally two functional interfaces: the systems' external interface to the environment, the Phenomenon, and the internal interface with which the systems are able to think and deliberate, the Noumenon.

The Phenomenon[22] is the mind's connection to the external environment, which is not only the physical world around the autonomous system, but also the physical world inside the autonomous system itself.

The Noumenon[23]—*das Ding des Denkens*, or the "thing of thinking"—is the internal system of the mind of the autonomous system. It is where all thinking takes place and where the cognitive functions are performed.

The Phenomenon and Noumenon are best described as "environments" as opposed to systems or subsystems because they represent true worlds unto themselves. This is one of the reasons Hegel went into the rewriting of the *Science of Logic* and delved into quantum and the invention of "the negation of the negation." In this sense, the Phenomenon and Noumenon are without limitation or constraint; these "meta-systems" of the mind pervade the entire autonomous system.

9.6 THE BUILDING OF PREFERENCES

Since humans and all biological beings possess a Will, individual survival is the principal attribute; thus, food or nourishment comes at the top of the Will's needs. Food in this case is energy because that is what food is processed into by the digestive system. In a mechanical system, energy is provided by fuel. For space exploration, such as that performed by the Voyager spacecraft, this energy or power would be provided by a radioisotope thermoelectric generator (RTG) using radioactive fuel. However, even this will be depleted eventually.

The Voyagers are automated in that they have predict files and are programmed by us to perform certain functions when the need arises, that is, by notifying the project team through radio transmissions what the problem is in a spacecraft state file. This helps only for a first step, but it does not help in identifying a set of steps that evolve into tastes, desires, repulsions, preferences, and so on, because it is not self-generated or self-programmed. Thus, the Voyagers are automated, not autonomous.

9.6.1 Illustration of Building Preferences

What follows is a brief discussion of building tastes and preferences with application to an autonomous system forced to use alternate fuels as an energy source.

There were many interesting inventions in Germany during the 1930s. One particularly interesting invention was the conversion of the internal combustion engine to use fuels other than gasoline. Since Germany has virtually no domestically available oil, the Standard Oil Company provided Germany with the Standard Oil-owned patent for converting coal into gasoline. The new German corporation, called Braunkohle-Benzin A.G., built several coal-to-gasoline conversion plants from 1935 to 1937. This, however, was not adequate to meet the energy needs of the German military and industry.

The Braunkohle-Benzin Corporation mass-produced a small one-quarter-ton all-electric truck, a three-wheeler. It worked well but needed to be charged when not in use. Collectively, this placed an unsupportable load on the hydroelectric and thermoelectric power plants supplying power for factory and civilian use.

This scenario provided the inspiration, the genius of an invention, in this case for a unique type of engine modification.

The engine modification was called a *Sauggasmotor*,[24] and allowed the motor to run on wood chips, charcoal, and *gas-koks* or *braunkohlen-koks* (small egg-shaped "pacquettes" that burn well in stoves), and larger coal briquettes made of anthracite or bituminous coal and other combustible materials.

A fully loaded 5-ton truck with the Sauggasmotor had a range of 100 km if provided with 100 kg of wood chips or 50 kg of coal (the mileage would vary with the kind of coal used, such as anthracite or bituminous). The smoke and gas were inducted from the fuel generator through the carburetors into the cylinder heads to be burned there, resulting in an essentially emission- and pollution-free system.

Similarly, the autonomous system, based on such performance factors, can easily develop preferences and adapt itself to them, especially when facing issues of survival.

Modeling the attributes of desires, the attractiveness[25] or repulsiveness of an object, fear,[26] the drive for survival through fear and the will to live,[27] and even beauty[28] (e.g., mathematics as feelings of beauty in nature) is not difficult with the state-of-the-art technology and mathematical tools available to the modern software systems engineer.

CHAPTER 10

The Architecture of the Thought System

The functional essence of the Thought system is the Noumenon, which integrates into itself the process and architecture of thought and thinking. The idea and concept for this architecture come from a synthesis of the total referenced works of Kant, Hegel, and Schopenhauer as interpreted by the authors. It is also heavily based on software project experience with human and spacecraft communication.

The role of the Thought system is to enable the autonomous system to be self-aware and self-conscious. This is the system that enables contemplation, analysis, internal dialogue, monologue, conferencing, broadcasting, and multifaceted discussions of issues of importance to any and all of the systems of the autonomous system. It permits the ability of the autonomous system to communicate internally, with and among itself, and externally, with humans as well as with other autonomous systems. This system is the actualization of the dictum of René Descartes's "*cogito, ergo sum*" and Kant's "*cogito, ergo est.*"

Hegel states, "Thinking is a process and a form, empty of content."[1] This statement, when read by a modern computer scientist or systems architect, has a far broader meaning than when it was written. It means that the Thought system is an architecture whether in use or not; it also means that its architecture depends on the time and discipline involved in building it. The Thought system, being a form, is thus a thing unto itself.

The Autonomous System: A Foundational Synthesis of the Sciences of the Mind,
First Edition. Szabolcs Michael de Gyurky and Mark A. Tarbell.
© 2014 John Wiley & Sons, Inc. Published 2014 by John Wiley & Sons, Inc.

Form, as used in this instance, is the network. When one adds content to the network, the content becomes *communication*. Communication means thinking, internally in the mind or Noumenon, and includes all of the forms of thought, including the Idea and Concept. The question often arises of the largest network in existence—the Internet—and if/when it will attain "consciousness," "self-awareness," "sentience," or some other form of transcendent behavior as more and more systems, nodes, and "smart" devices are added to it. The answer to this fanciful question is that the Internet has the *wrong architecture* for autonomy. *It is only with the infusion of the mental (conscious) involvement of human beings that the Internet can take on an outward impression of consciousness.* The Internet *unto itself* is simply a distributed repository for abstract content, and any "process" or "form" that may be observed[2] is that which is imposed upon it by its users from without; *it has no volition or Will of its own.* Thus, the Internet is inherently incapable of thought and will remain so, regardless of size or number of "neurons" connected to it. Hegel deals with this phenomenon in detail in his *Science of Logic* and *Science of Being*, to which the reader is referred.

10.1 THE "MOVERS" OF THE THOUGHT PROCESS

The Thought system subsumes the myriad functions that a communication system would perform; they are combined into one system, the Noumenon. An immediate reason for this is that the functions they perform are very tightly coupled and often overlap.

The role of a communication system is that of the functional communications center of the autonomous system: it monitors, queues, switches, assigns, and reassigns the task and performance responsibilities of the autonomous system. It controls the external communications from the sensors of the autonomous system (which are via the Phenomenon monads) and the internal communications between the systems (which are via the Noumenon monads). These monads carry the information uninterruptedly through the autonomous system's constellation.

Another reason for combining the Thought and Communication systems is the problem of dealing with the placement of two very critical functions: the Idea (*Idee*) and the Concept (*Begriff*). These two functions form a significant part of the work of Arthur Schopenhauer, G.F.W. Hegel, and Immanuel Kant. It is not the scope of the two functions alone that makes them large and complex, but their significance to the thought process. Schopenhauer looks at this problem from one angle; Hegel and Kant slightly differently. However, all three agree on the importance of "the Idea as a function" as a construct, which looms large in the human thought system. Schopenhauer considers it so important that he actually postulates that the "only function of the Reason is to generate the Concept."[3] However, this is not an elegant or feasible design approach from the software architectural point of view.

The Reason by its very nature is the primary "gainsayer" of the Will. It challenges the Will in many of its "want-to-dos." It informs the Will when it is not in line with the laws or rules that it has set for itself.[4] If the laws set by the Will through experience are transgressed or ignored, this will lead to the eventual destruction of the autonomous system or serious damage to the system constellation. The process of generating an Idea is considered the most important and unique attribute of the mind of a human being. It is the one that separates it from the purely biological animals, and as such is the first prime mover of the thought process.

The Concept (*Begriff*) is the other prime mover of the thought process. It is a processor and a mental design object in time and space. It is generated by the initial stimulation of the Idea,[5] and indeed it is for our design purposes an extension of the Idea and often remains a mental image object. Immanuel Kant considers the Idea a Concept of the Reason in his *Kritik der reinen Vernunft*, and bases his development of the Idea on Plato's works. It can and should become an object projected onto the Presentation system for viewing and discussion by all of the systems in the constellation. In the Presentation of a well-developed human mind, it can progress to a well-defined and rational Concept. In human beings, this may happen only if the mind of the thinker is equipped with the Intellect, Understanding, and Decision necessary to complete the substantiation process. Additionally, the Presentation system must also be very highly developed. In the case of the design of the autonomous system's software architecture, this is not as issue of philosophy but one of design necessity.

Hegel, however, has a somewhat different place for the Idea. He postulates that the Idea is pure Understanding, and Logic is pure science. It is described broadly in the original German.[6]

For our purposes, the Idea can originate in any of the Will, Reason, or Understanding systems, but it is up to the Nexus Cogitationis to develop it into a Concept. This design approach is necessary for design efficiency and may be modified. We must keep in mind that Kant, Hegel, and Schopenhauer were philosopher-scientists, not 21st-century computer scientists. The autonomous system itself is a Concept based on their Ideas.

The Thought and Communication system is key to the understanding of the autonomous system, its functional design and requirements, and its operation. This is where thought and communication take place; *they are inseparable*. It is important to understand that there will be no autonomous system unless it can think in human language. Therefore, there are no shortcuts in the skills required by the manager-architect, systems engineer, and the members of the design team undertaking the building of an autonomous system. The thorough understanding of languages, mathematics, logic, and philosophy is required. As a science, thinking has long been a point of great interest and study among scientists and scholars—in fact, since the time of Aristotle. One issue is clear: An autonomous system must be able to think, speak, contemplate, make rational decisions, and act on these decisions. Anything less does not an autonomous system make.

10.2 THE PURSUIT OF THINKING

In 1658, the great Spanish thinker Baltasar Gracian made a wonderful observation on philosophy, thinking, and knowledge. It is worth to quote it in its entirety for a better understanding of the entire autonomous system structure as seen from the perspective of the people who would consider building it.

> *Too much time is spent on the pursuit of wealth, too little on the thinking spirit. With limited exception, philosophy, built on a system of truth, stands discredited today, even though it was once the major pursuit of the sages. In today's generation, there appears to be little time available beyond the pursuit of wealth and pleasure. Forgotten is the pleasure found in the art of thinking clearly or in deductive reasoning to gain knowledge. The tools of philosophy—reason, observation, and intuition—lie rusted in sad ruins as the world speeds through the universe in search of itself. Although the science of thinking lives in loneliness, and at times is even degraded, it is to be noted that the question of how man acquires knowledge and learns truth is ever*

the food of the thinking spirit, and the joy of the high-minded and respectable.[7]

10.3 THE NEXUS COGITATIONIS

***nexus**: ūs,* m. *necto,*[8]
– a tying or binding together, a fastening, joining, an interlacing, entwining, clasping.

***cōgĭtātionis**: ūs,* f. *cogito, co-agito*[9]
– a thinking, thought, reflection, meditation
– the faculty of thought

The Thought system is the system to be addressed last because it contains the *Nexus Cogitationis*—the fulcrum of the mind of the autonomous system and its ability to think and communicate. The Nexus initiates self-awareness and consciousness. It directs, tracks, and organizes all physical and speculative operations. It is the communication system/subsystem that contains speech, mathematical operations, and logic. It is where the systems of the mind of the constellation are initialized.

The Nexus Cogitationis emerged as a subsystem to the Noumenon because the Will and the Reason systems are not sufficient in themselves to do what a human being of high intelligence does. The Will, being the metaphysical *prius*, broadens itself out through experience driven by survival, reproduction, and dominance of its space or environment. The lowliest living thing has a Will, yet with the human being at the apex, it is necessary for design that there be something even more fundamentally primary in the human mind beyond the Will and the Reason.

In the process of survival, reproduction, and dominance, the Will system learns lessons through its successes and mistakes, and creates laws according to what it needs and does not need, what it must do and must not do. Once achieved, this learning by making positive experiences or by making mistakes becomes a flood of Sensory system input, providing input for contemplation, decision, and database-building activity. The positive or negative object, action, or phenomenon is presented to the Imagination system internally for the contemplation and analysis of the systems in the constellation. When the analysis is rigorous, thorough, and driven home to a rational conclusion, it is filed with the Intellect system, if there is one already. If there is not, an Intellect system is created provisionally, and upon further input and effort, is finalized.

First, we must *visualize*—the *Anschauung* that Kant discusses so extensively—and obtain the *a priori* impression of this unique thing or *Ding*, and inferentially discuss what we are looking at inwardly in our minds. Then we get to the gate of Hegel's logic and all that this implies for us who are visualizing the Thought system.

"Logic is the science of thinking,"[10] and as such it is shown by Hegel that thinking is an architectural activity, imaginary with a real form and operational attributes, with the postulate that it is a "form," a "thing empty of contents,"[11] based on a discrete recognition. What makes it so very difficult for many human beings to describe is that the individuals attempting to understand it can do so only with a personal attribute termed by Kant as *Einbildungsvermögen*. In short, this German word means "imagination assets." Thus, the person possessing it owns the full capacity to receive a complete mental impression of a physical or imaginary object, the imaginary object being a product of the mind, *a priori*.

There are several overarching principles involved in the Thought system. The first is monumental, and we will quote it in the original German because of its importance and relevance here. "*Wahrheit ist die Übereinstimmung des Denkens mit dem Gegenstand*"[12] or "Truth is the unqualified agreement of the Thought with the object." This is one of the reasons for design purposes we have established the constellation of the mind as a grouping of individual and distinct systems. It would be impossibly complicated to design and build, with our current state of the art, an autonomous system in the context we are discussing here composed on a single system.

All of the systems of the human mind, except for the Will, are defined, registered, and developed by the human individual who possesses the willpower, discipline, and tenacity to study, listen, and learn and who drives himself from early infancy to develop himself and strives for knowledge and experience. Without this terribly demanding effort, the mind cannot produce systems like an Intellect, an Understanding, or a Reason.

There are circumstances when a person may have these systems but in a very underdeveloped form due to neglect. Some have incomplete and underdeveloped minds and constellations. Unfortunately, as Schopenhauer claimed, except for their outward biological forms and appearances, they are no different from a primate in terms of intellectual and reasoning capacity.

The basic laws of thinking are recognition, connection, conclusion, and verdict.[13] The verdict on truth in this case is not based on empirical or metaphysical data, but on the logic of Being, *Seinslogik*, and the structure of mass logic, *Maßlogik*, or "metalogic," which makes interfaces, connections, and relationships easier to understand and to use.

10.4 THE SUBSYSTEMS OF THE THOUGHT SYSTEM

The Thought system has three subsystems:

- The Nexus Cogitationis subsystem
- The Communication subsystem
- The Network subsystem.

These three subsystems belong to the sphere of the Noumenon. The primary external interface of the Thought system with the Phenomenon is through the Communication subsystem, and then through the Sensory subsystem, which provides physical impressions from the environment.

10.4.1 The Nexus Cogitationis Subsystem

The Nexus Cogitationis is the central operator, controller, organizer, orchestrator, and monitor of the thought process in the mind of the autonomous system. It is the collective "I" as opposed to the subjective "me" of the Will. The Nexus, at least from this design point of view, is where the process of thinking begins in the autonomous system. "I think" is an empirical rule containing the state "I exist,"[14] taken from the famous statement by Descartes' "*cogito*"—"I think." The "I" in this rule is purely intellectual because it belongs to the thought process. Without any empirical presentation, which provides the material for making thinking possible, the *actus* (motion-force-state) *cogito* is not possible. The relationship between the Nexus and the systems is one based on the environmental input from the Phenomenon. The "I" cannot exist without the outside world of the senses.[15]

The Logic program set is pure thought. As applied to a system, it must be learned first so that one can gain a clear understanding of the meaning of things. In the autonomous system, the Logic program set is designed from the start so that the autonomous system will be a logical thinker.[16] The system of logic concerns itself with the object and its contents, and is thought through and processed using dialectics and rhythm.[17] Logic has two processes, the primary being elementary logic, and the secondary applied logic. It is sufficient here to say only that applied logic is what is taught today in curricula requiring an understanding of logic. This logic has lost the great frame of material substance that in earlier days made it a science.

The design objective in providing logic as a property to the autonomous system is to bestow it with the ability to think logically, clearly, and accurately, which implies that the autonomous system requires, in the long run, elementary logic. Elementary logic means the fulfillment of all truth, and to provide the truth with a universal value.

The entire logical structure of the language as used to think internally and communicate externally should reside in the Nexus. When the autonomous system communicates and manifests action, it should be in the form of an advanced, human language. In the engineering disciplines, we communicate in mathematical forms and logic diagrams almost as much as we do in speech. In some instances, using logic diagrams, dataflow/relationship/process charts, and mathematics, we overcome the linguistic limitations of some of our colleagues. With an autonomous system that is involved in the exploration of deep space, all forms of communications should be considered. The selection of modes of communication will be at the initiative of the Nexus.

The Contemplation program set is the equivalent mental activity of the entire mind of the constellation without external sensory input.

The Nexus Cogitationis is not only the orchestrator and controller of the Thought system, but it plays the dominant role in the software architecture. To leave the functions assigned to it in the Will or the Reason systems would mean that the Nexus would become either too physically primitive in its operation or too constrained in axioms, rules, and laws. This would make the all-important development of Concepts (*Begriffe*) narrowly oriented and unbalanced in scope, that is, totally legal and moral, or totally physical- and survival-driven, as in animals and many humans. In other words, if the development of the Concept were in the Reason system, then the system constellation would be an automaton, a total slave of axioms, rules, and laws. If it were placed in the Will system, it would become no more than an animal, since nature knows only the physical and not the higher moral laws that humans need to live together in a society. In most human beings, all practical (moral) direction comes through the Reason.

We need a "dominant I" that is balanced sufficiently enough to at least mimic a free will, although this may not be possible. We start with what a modern computer scientist would never have thought of as an important or even relevant book in the architecture of an advanced autonomous system. This masterwork is G.W.F. Hegel's *Wissenschaft der Logik, Die Lehre vom Sein* (1832, two books combined). This is probably best translated as *The Science of Logic* and *The Science of Being*. *The Science of Logic* is a natural fit for computer software architecture; *The Science of Being* is not, at least at first glance. It took many years of background processing in the mind to discover how important the concept of Being (*Sein*) is in computer science. Hegel puts it this way: "The Concept, when it has developed into a concrete existence that is itself free, is none other than the 'I,' which is pure self consciousness."[18]

Any system that is capable of thinking, contemplation, analysis, decision, and action must have an *identity*. This is necessary because an autonomous system must be capable of and have the vital attribute of *self–nonself discrimination*. This is an essential part of the cognitive attributes of an autonomous system. Without this attribute, it will not be able to discriminate logically between the outside world (the Phenomenon) and the inside world (itself, the Noumenon or Thought system). We provide self–nonself-discrimination to an autonomous system not only for its own ability to know who it is, but also to initialize the all-important process of Being (see §10.5).

10.4.2 The Communication Subsystem

The Communication subsystem is one of the great conceptual software engineering undertakings or enterprises of the mind of the autonomous system. It is unique in that it operates simultaneously on several levels, such as human language mode, physical sensor mode, and thought mode. It is a synthesis of sounds, symbols, characters, grammar, vocabulary, mathematics, and elementary logic.

The Human Language program set is the first consideration in the design and construction of an autonomous system.[19] Therefore, we must select and provide to the autonomous system a very advanced and highly developed language in which to think internally and communicate externally. With such a language, there must not be ambiguities or misunderstandings in the process of the task of survival and solving problems. We know that mathematics[20] is the primary tool for the human interface with the physical and mechanical world. Hegel points out that the first to accomplish the transliteration of human philosophical concepts from human language into mathematical form was Pythagoras.[21] It seems that we in computer science have always ignored Hegel and his fabulous book on Being.[22] It should be well read and on the bookshelf of all serious software engineers.

The Language program set must do the same as Pythagoras did, performing a transliteration of the ideas in mathematical expressions to the selected human language, and vice versa. There must be a complete lexicon of words, their types, usages, and relationships and linkages within sentence structures and their usage in science and engineering operations. This is governed by mathematical form. This will ensure a rigorous, precise usage of the language, without slang or substandard construction. This is but one possible way for the constellation of the mind of the autonomous system to communicate both internally and externally using human language.

The Physical Sensor program set translates the raw data processed by the Sensory system into human language, mathematical terms, figures, forms, symbols and relationships, and graphical linkage relationships and representations. These objects are projected onto the Presentation system and undergo an analysis process that will add substance to the objects being viewed. This process is an unending activity and occurs at an ever higher input rate until the objects being viewed have exhausted the material necessary to as completely and accurately as possible conclude and round out their nomenclature. This is an incredibly dynamic environment as far as transactions, processing, storage, and retrieval are concerned. Only with the help of Hegel's dynamic logic and his quantum can a good software systems architect visualize the physical and intellectual architecture.

10.4.3 The Network Subsystem

The Network subsystem for design purposes is the information network of the systems of the constellation. The information in this case is exchanged in human language, because we humans think in language. The cultural development of human beings is dependent on the advanced organization, grammar, vocabulary size, and precision of the syntax of the languages a particular society uses. Simple languages cannot be used to think in complex technical terms or to solve technical problems. The Network subsystem is, like the Thought system as a whole, an empty architecture. It is like a telephone network without traffic, to use Hegel's analogy. It must be *used* in order to have substance. In order to simplify the huge amount of information presented by Hegel and Schopenhauer, we are presenting it in its process design format.

From a systems architectural position, the Thought system or Noumenon is composed of a network whose modes of interaction are dedicated to the following four types.

10.4.3.1 The Monologue

The Monologue program set mode is designed for the Nexus Cogitationis to address each system separately to update its organization and functions. It also serves as a mode for any system to address another directly with information required by the target system. One of these addresses may consist of an information fragment placed on the Presentation system for general information. Another might be the direct response by the Reason system to the Will to inform it to cease attempting to initiate an action that is against an established law, axiom, or rule.

This is a tool used by a system to transmit, without being interrupted, information about its internal interest and position. This is referred to as "reflection on a theme." In the advanced, well-educated human mind, it would be analogous to the Reason holding forth an interpretation on a certain theme, such as some aspect of ethics. One such aspect might be on an issue of whether it is appropriate to have a certain law or axiom, such as obeying an uplinked command from the Space Flight Operations Facility (SFOC) or not. The monologue for this example, as a reflection on a theme, would be internal to the Reason system and the Nexus Cogitationis, and would not directly involve the other systems because it needs no response.

10.4.3.2 The Broadcast

The Broadcast program set is the program set mode that informs all the systems in the constellation to take note of an event in process that is important for the entire constellation. One such event is the presentation of new phenomena on the Presentation system. An example would be that the Sensory system (i.e., Phenomenon) has detected a change in temperature or radio emission from a source in space. As it broadcasts this information, the Intellect system might provide data to the Understanding system that this phenomenon is most likely a radiation burst from a nearby star. The Presentation system would collect all information pertaining to these phenomena and present the completed picture to the constellation. The Will system might then make the final countermeasure course of action to prevent damage to any of the systems. All of the *a posteriori* information is packaged by the Nexus and sent to the Understanding system, where these are filed in the Form of All Appearances and Form of All Possibilities subsystems.

10.4.3.3 The Dialogue

The Dialogue program set mode is used in situations in which the Decision system is in the process of establishing a preference or making a ruling or a verdict on an object, event, or process. This starts as a proposition in the Broadcast mode to the Intellect and Understanding systems. The resulting Dialogue takes place in a freewheeling debate between the Intellect and Understanding systems. The former has the knowledge, which may be abstract, experiential, or real; the latter has the form of all appearances and the form of all possibilities that are beneficial or harmful to the constellation.

Such a process might initiate when, for example, the Will system is queried as to whether the survival of the autonomous system as an entity outweighs the commands it has received externally (e.g., from Earth). This could happen if, for whatever hypothetical reason, the SFOC wished to terminate the spacecraft and cancel the mission (such as was done when the Galileo spacecraft was commanded to plunge itself into Jupiter). The response of the Will system would be that which forms the basis for the existence of the original mission objectives and the reasoning behind them, ethics aside.

10.4.3.4 The Conference

The Conference program set mode is a direct engagement undertaken prior to a decision, judgment, verdict, or preference concerning an object, event, or phenomenon. The Conference is often due not to Sensory input but to a mental process while the thinking takes place. One such process is the phenomenon in which a human being is in the process of trying to solve a problem, becomes tired of expending willful thought on it, and "sleeps on it." This type of transaction is considered a type of background processing in which a problem is solved without primary resources being directly allocated to its solving. This type of thinking and contemplation especially intrigued Kant and Schopenhauer.

A Conference takes place with the Nexus Cogitationis in contemplation, going through in great detail all *a priori* events and all *a posteriori* conclusions, proven or not.

All of these are available and shared equally by all of the systems in the constellation of the mind. All of the systems follow set rules that are under the control of the Nexus Cogitationis as described above.

Thus, from a computer science architectural point of view, and equally from the software engineering perspective, we have had to invent the Nexus Cogitationis and to make it a system that would better fit its critical position in the architecture.

10.5 INITIALIZATION PROCESS OF THE AUTONOMOUS SYSTEM

The initialization process or genesis of the autonomous system is critical because it forms the baseline of self-awareness and imagination. In human beings, as in all biological systems, self–nonself-discrimination is the first to develop in the Will. In human beings, it has the additional step of *Becoming* (*Werden*), and then *Being* (*Sein*). This follows in what Kant, Hegel, and Schopenhauer describe as *Moments*. This is fortunate for us because there are no other viable models to follow if we wish to obtain human-like results. These great thinkers have done the groundbreaking work for the design of the autonomous system.

When the cognitive functions have been programmed, tested, and integrated, one can see that the Nexus Cogitationis is akin to what we used to call "situation monitoring."

Using the nomenclature of Hegel, there is initially *Pure Nothing*. The process that is about to take place is called *Becoming*.

When the autonomous system is instantiated, the sequence in the Nexus Cogitationis plays out as follows.

10.5.1 Before the First Moment

State: *Pure Nothing*
Result: Intention of *Becoming*
Description: Pure Nothing is the starting and the end point of all things in the cognitive world. There is no object without a subject, and no existence without the environment, the Phenomenon. Thus, this is not a "Determinate Nothing," but the conceptual "Pure Nothing" of Hegel.

10.5.2 The Becoming

State: *Initialization*
Result: Intention of initialization is instantiated
Description: This is the *Becoming*, the "zeroth moment," the "desire to initialize self" process of the autonomous system constellation.

10.5.3 First Moment

State: *Determinate Nothing* (concept of *"I"* emerges)
Result: The Nexus Cogitationis is instantiated
Description: The Nexus Cogitationis (unto itself, the *subject*) brings itself into being and is in a suspended state. Recall that without an *Object*, there is no *Subject*, as there are yet no other systems, including the Communication system. The Nexus Cogitationis, however, being the control center, has within its instantiation a communication modality called the *Noumena band*. The Communication System is the normal location for external and internal communications interfaces, called the *Phenomena band*. Until the Communication system is instantiated in the Eighth Moment (§10.5.10), the Nexus will communicate with the nascent systems as each comes online through the *bands of the Noumena*.

10.5.4 Second Moment

State: *Something* (concept of *self* emerges)
Result: The Will system is instantiated
Description: The Will system, which is the metaphysical *prius* and a totally physical, survival-oriented system, exerts itself and notifies the

Nexus Cogitationis in a monologue mode that it is present. The Nexus Cogitationis replies, also in a monologue mode,[23] that it has recognized the Will system, and the Will system is registered with the Individual Survival subsystem, the Survival of the Species subsystem, and the Dominance subsystem.

10.5.5 Third Moment

State: *Something Else* (concept of *nonself* emerges)
Result: The Sensory system is instantiated
Description: The Sensory system addresses the Nexus Cogitationis in a monologue mode, providing the first burst of sensory data from the nearest (or most immediate) object in the Phenomenon. The Nexus Cogitationis replies that it recognizes the Sensory system and that it is registered with the Internal Sensory program sets: the Sensory Data Processing program set, the External Sensory Data program set (the Phenomenon: external data input), the Sensory Data Records program set, and the Experiment Data Records program set.[24]

(It must be noted here that in the event of a requirements and implementation phase, more program sets may be added. The number of program sets depends on the scope of the final product expected by the sponsor. Note also that an autonomous system designed for interplanetary exploration, or for establishing a Mission Support Site (MSS) on a planet, will require many more program sets than a network security system or a medical or biological analysis system. There is no simple or short workaround to bypass JPL-STD-D-4000.)

10.5.6 Fourth Moment

State: *Something More*
Result: The Reason system is instantiated
Description: The Reason system addresses the Nexus Cogitationis in a dialogue mode. It describes its readiness for receiving its subsystems' definitions and data inputs. The Nexus Cogitationis replies that it recognizes the Reason system and that it is registered with the Laws subsystem, the Rules subsystem, and the Axioms subsystem. It is also linked instantly in a dialogue mode with the Will system for emergency input and response, as in the case of survival events. In human beings and animals, this process starts at conception. In the autonomous

systems constellation, this is initialization and linkage with an already programmed and tested system (i.e., a system in the constellation that has undergone the rigorous test and integration phase as specified in JPL-STD-D-4000.[25] More precisely, any system, such as the Reason or the Understanding, must have been completed and fully tested before the constellation level instantiation can begin. This requirement applies to the Thought system and Nexus Cogitationis also.)

10.5.7 Fifth Moment

State: *Something More*
Result: The Intellect system is instantiated
Description: The Nexus Cogitationis addresses the Intellect system in a dialogue mode. It queries the Intellect system as to its readiness to receive the download of data required by the Intellect to generate knowledge. It requests a read-back of the status of its Abstract subsystem, its Experience subsystem, and its Knowledge subsystem. This process initializes the relationship of the Intellect with the other systems of the constellation.

It must be understood that there is no real knowledge (practical knowledge) unless/until the abstract data are validated by experience. If there is no experience, then when information is needed for action or use, the request defaults to the Abstract subsystem. In cases where there is experience with abstract data, but the two have not yet been integrated into knowledge, the experience takes precedence during the selection process. Experience, whether gained hands-on or through close participation and observation, is the dominant type of practical knowledge data.

10.5.8 Sixth Moment

State: *Something More*
Result: The Understanding system is instantiated
Description: The Nexus Cogitationis addresses the Understanding system in a dialogue mode. It queries the Understanding system as to its readiness to receive the downloading of the data it needs to perform its function. This includes the data formats and information fragments large and small to populate its Form of All Appearances and Form of All Possibilities subsystems. In the process of forming an Idea or

Concept, this system draws on the instantiated systems of the constellation in a broadcast mode for the data it needs to complete the data sets required in formulating its possibilities.

10.5.9 Seventh Moment

State: *Awareness* starts
Result: The Presentation system is instantiated
Description: The Nexus Cogitationis addresses the Presentation system in a broadcast mode. It queries the Presentation system as to its readiness to accept the download of the input from the instantiated systems in the constellation, and of compiling and arranging the fragments or parts of visual, audio, graphical, mass, motion, and other data into a single object for analysis. This whole or partially complete object is updated instantly by the constellation simultaneously. In highly intelligent human beings, this occurs instantly and dynamically. In others it occurs sequentially, hierarchically, slowly; hence the term, "slow of wit," the result of the neglect to build one's brain and develop mental capacity and effort for thinking. Note that it is often camouflaged by fast reflexes (which bypass the Thought and Decision systems) and autonomic, animal-like responses to stimuli. It is only through training, discipline, and practice that in humans the mind becomes large and able to process huge amounts of data to build a complete object for viewing. The systems of the constellation at this time channel all relevant data in their possession to the Presentation system for completing the object.

10.5.10 Eighth Moment

State: *Awareness* continues to develop
Result: The Communication subsystem is instantiated
Description: The Nexus Cogitationis addresses in a monologue mode the Communication subsystem of the Thought system. It queries the Communication subsystem as to its readiness to convert sensory and contemplative data into mathematical equations, into human language, and all other forms and methods and parts of communication. It is also asked to validate the language it has been given for use, its grammatical rules, syllogisms, and syntax. When this has been accomplished, the Communication subsystem will address the constellation in a broadcast mode and provide each system with the selected human language to be

used in thinking internally and communicating externally. This is followed by a conference mode exchange in which the language selected is discussed and tested by the constellation for adaptability to the applications toward which the constellation is to be put, and the problems the constellation needs to solve.

10.5.11 Ninth and Final Moment

State: *Being* (awareness is established)
Result: The Decision system is instantiated
Description: The Nexus Cogitationis addresses the Decision system in a monologue mode as to its readiness to evaluate and select preferences, likes and dislikes, and its ability to make decisions based on all input received from Sensory External data, and from input received from the other systems in the constellation.

10.5.12 Initialized State

At this point, we have a nascent yet functioning system constellation replicating at a Level I the way in which the cognitive functions of the autonomous system can work. The thinking and contemplating process is now self-capable of the continued building of its cognitive abilities and decision-making abilities. It is a never-ending and ever expansive process.

To place this into Hegelian perspective:

> *The object therefore has its objectivity in the Concept and this is the unity of self-consciousness into which it has been received; consequently its objectivity, or the Concept, is itself none other than the nature of self-consciousness, has no other moments or determinations than the I itself.*[26]

Epilogue

We have reached the completion of a long road of discovery, learning, and experience in computer science. Above all, we have completed what the sages called a *Verstandesbegriff*,[1] a "concept of the Understanding." Indeed, thinking—*pure thinking*—is considered a system of concepts. Logic is in turn the science of pure thinking.[2] Thus, in the design of the autonomous system, we can originate concepts from the Reason, the Intellect, and even the Presentation. In this book, we have set down the synthesis of the information received from the systems that form the constellation of the human mind. The mind, therefore, must be considered as software, for it contains the equivalent of operating systems, applications, and other dedicated processes. The brain by definition is hardware, with its capacity to accommodate and execute software. The Idea[3] is from the human mind, and is therefore mental as opposed to cerebral or physical.

The intent of this journey was at first innocent. A former director of the Jet Propulsion Laboratory (JPL) simply requested a paradigm shift—the next "big idea"—from the staff. He wanted something for JPL that was totally new to pursue and work on. It was just coincidental that at that very time, the first author was reading Immanuel Kant's *Critique of Pure Reason*[4] and working on a spacecraft telemetry, command, and communication system under an impossibly tight schedule and an equally impossible budget.

Relaxing with Kant and trying to solve big problems means stress, which means an expansion of mental activity. This is the state that often produces unexpected leaps in science and engineering. Schopenhauer[5] calls this state "the forcible expansion of the mind";[6] he is not generous to those unwilling to go through the painful mental process required to achieve it.

It was an almost momentous "instant revelation of connectivity" type of discovery[7] that the works of Immanuel Kant were very relevant

The Autonomous System: A Foundational Synthesis of the Sciences of the Mind,
First Edition. Szabolcs Michael de Gyurky and Mark A. Tarbell.
© 2014 John Wiley & Sons, Inc. Published 2014 by John Wiley & Sons, Inc.

to modern computer science, leading to the organization of a new approach of doing software design and implementation.[8] The successful delivery of a quality software product in time for the launching of a spacecraft reinforced the awareness of the *imperative* connection between cognitive philosophy and modern computer science.

The fact that the spacecraft system mentioned earlier ended up being extremely well documented and fully tested, without any delivery slips, aroused even greater interest in cognitive philosophy as a tool to better understanding computer software. The reading of Hegel's *Science of Logic* and *Science of Being* brought into focus the idea that *computer software is an abstraction of the human thought system*. Arthur Schopenhauer's great work, *The World as Will and Presentation*, was a natural for understanding the organization and operation of the human Will and its interfaces with the Reason, the Understanding, and the Intellect. The resulting discovery of the connectivity to philosophy and its meaning led to the examination of the ongoing work in artificial intelligence and the efforts to come up with an architecture of a machine that could think and act independently of human direction.

It is a strange feeling to have completed this book, knowing that this is just the beginning of a new appreciation for computer science *as a science*. Indeed, it is just a small step in the continuous evolution of a great science as it takes its rightful place amid the others. There are new worlds of the mind to explore because computer science incorporates all of the sciences that involve the human thought system, its development and training process: logic, mathematics, ontology, rational psychology, cosmology, speculative philosophy, dialectic reasoning, music, art, and so on.[9]

We now have a new insight into why we have heretofore not been able to build an autonomous system, why we have been stopped in our pursuit of autonomy short of our goals. The preparation of this book reveals a very interesting phenomenon, in fact a startling truth that leads back to Hegel and Schopenhauer. This new truth is that computer science ultimately is made up of *two* segments: The first segment comprises the physical or "empirical" sciences, while the second and complementary segment comprises the metaphysical sciences, such as logic, mathematics, and ontology (being). The sciences of the mind and the way we think play an indispensable role in how we model and replicate the process of dynamic thought.

Thus we have arrived, with the help of computer science rediscovered, at a foundational synthesis of the sciences of the human mind.

Endnotes

NOTES FOR PREFACE

1 From "On the Method of Theoretical Physics" (The Herbert Spencer Lecture, Oxford, June 10, 1933).
2 G.W.F. Hegel, *Wissenschaft der Logik, Die Lehre vom Sein* (1832) (Hamburg: Felix Meiner Verlag, 1990), 300–350.
3 I.S. Gradstein, I.H. Ryshik, *Tafeln: Tables of Series, Products, and Integrals* (1981), vols. 1 and 2 (Frankfurt: Verlag Harri Deutsch, 1981).
4 Hegel, *Wissenschaft der Logik, Die Lehre vom Sein*, 226–235.
5 Szabolcs M. de Gyurky, *The Cognitive Dynamics of Computer Science* (Hoboken, NJ: John Wiley & Sons, 2006).

NOTES FOR INTRODUCTION

1 *JPL-Software Management Standard D-4000*, Version 3.0 (Pasadena, CA: Jet Propulsion Laboratory, California Institute of Technology, December 1988). This standard is ideally suited for the analysis and preproject functional requirements planning phase of a system of the scope and complexity presented in this book.
2 The autonomous system cannot be programmed using modern "fly-by-the-pants" implementation techniques. Fortunately, such complex systems could, however, be programmed using a radically new systems development, testing, and integration technique presented by a holographic computational system and methodology concept.
3 An optional part of this prerequisite is the strong desirability of understanding with native fluency the language these works were written in—not the modern German or English language translations used in the classrooms, but the Old German in which they were published originally. Languages change naturally enough over time, and many words lose or permute their meanings or are dropped because of the difficulty modern readers have in understanding multiple, often simultaneously contradictory meanings.

The Autonomous System: A Foundational Synthesis of the Sciences of the Mind,
First Edition. Szabolcs Michael de Gyurky and Mark A. Tarbell.
© 2014 John Wiley & Sons, Inc. Published 2014 by John Wiley & Sons, Inc.

4 Immanuel Kant, *Kritik der reinen Vernunft*, Herausgegeben und eingeleitet von August Messer (Berlin: Verlag von Th. Knaur Nachf, not dated, but circa 1924), xiii.

5 Arthur Schopenhauer, *Die Welt als Wille und Vorstellung*, Gesamtausgabe (Munich: Deutscher Taschenbuch Verlag GmbH & Co. KG, 1954), 23.

6 G.W.F. Hegel, *Die Lehre vom Sein* (Hamburg: Felix Meiner Verlag, 1990), 50.

7 Ibid., 102

8 Henri Pirenne, *Mohammed and Charlemagne*, English trans. Bernard Miall (London: George Allen & Unwin, 1954).

9 Arthur Schopenhauer, *Die Welt als Wille und Vorstellung*, Book Two (Munich: Deutscher Taschenbuch Verlag GmbH & Co. KG, 1998), 142.

10 Immanuel Kant, *Kritik der reinen Vernunft* (Riga: Johann Friedrich Hartknoch,1788; reprint, Berlin: Verlag von Th. Knaur Nachf., circa 1916), 201.

11 Schopenhauer, *Die Welt als Wille und Vorstellung* (1998), 81.

12 Szabolcs M. de Gyurky, *The Cognitive Dynamics of Computer Science* (Hoboken, NJ: John Wiley & Sons, 2006).

13 Plato, *The Republic, Works of Plato* (New York: Tudor Publishing, 1933), 75.

14 Kant, *Kritik der reinen Vernunft*.

15 G.W.F. Hegel, *Wissenschaft der Logik*, Part I; Objective Logic. Erster Band: Die Lehre vom Sein (Ontology) (Hamburg: Felix Meiner Verlag, 1990), 46.

16 Ibid., 280–298.

17 I.S. Gradstein and I.H. Ryshik, *Tafeln: Tables of Series, Products, and Integrals* (Frankfurt: Verlag Harri Deutsch, 1981), vols. 1 and 2.

18 de Gyurky, *The Cognitive Dynamics of Computer Science*.

19 Ibid., chap. 4.

20 Ibid., §4.12–4.15.

21 Ibid., chap. 9.

NOTES FOR CHAPTER 1

1 Arthur Schopenhauer, *Die Welt als Wille und Vorstellung* [The World as Will and Presentation] (Munich: Deutscher Taschenbuch Verlag GmbH & Co. KG, 1998), 7.

2 Arthur Schopenhauer, *Die Welt als Wille und Vorstellung* [The World as Will and Presentation], Drittes Buch (Book Three, esp. pp. 300–325 on the objects: the Idea, the Concept, and the Genius), Gesamtausgabe (Munich: Deutscher Taschenbuch Verlag GmbH & Co. KG, 1988).

3 Ibid.

4 Ibid.

5 Schopenhauer, *Die Welt als Wille und Vorstellung* (1998).

6 Szabolcs M. de Gyurky, *The Cognitive Dynamics of Computer Science* (Hoboken, NJ: John Wiley & Sons, 2006), §4.12–4.15.

7 Monads are a Level III implementation concern. The reader is referred to §18.8.2 in de Gyurky, *The Cognitive Dynamics of Computer Science*.

8 G.W.F. Hegel, *Wissenschaft der Logik, Die Lehre vom Sein* (Hamburg: Felix Meiner Verlag, 1832), 300–350.

9 See §10.4.3, The Network Subsystem, for a detailed description.

10 G.W.F. Hegel, *Die Lehre vom Sein* (Riga: Johann Friedrich Hartknoch, 1788), figure 3, The Science of Being.

11 Arthur Schopenhauer, *Die Welt als Wille und Vorstellung* (Munich: Gesamtausgabe. Deutscher Taschenbuch Verlag GmbH & Co. KG, 1954).

12 Ibid.

13 Thucydides. *The Peloponnesian War* (London: J. M. Dent; New York: E. P. Dutton, 1910), paraphrased.

14 Immanuel Kant, *Kritik der praktischen Vernunft* (reprint, Berlin-Leipzig: Verlag von Th. Knaur Nachf., circa 1916).

15 Ibid.

16 Ibid.

17 Ibid.

18 Arthur Schopenhauer, *The World as Will and Presentation: First Inspection/Die Welt als erste Betrachtung: Die Vorstellung unterworfen dem Saтze vom Grunde: Das Objekt der Erfahrung und Wissenschaft.*

19 Phenomenon monads are those that carry the sensory data from the external environment into the internal environment. It is the Noumenon monads that carry the internal communications data of the system.

20 Immanuel Kant, *Critique of Decisions and Verdict, Kritik Der Urteilskraft.* (Berlin: Legarde and Friedrich, 1792; reprint, Hamburg: Karl Vorländer, through Felix Meiner Publishers, 1954).

21 Over the course of a year, the first author studied (as an intellectual exercise) the large Mekong rats in their environment in the great swamp called the Rung Shat. Their large numbers and their individual and group behavior were ideal for study and experiment in an isolated U.S. Army Special Forces Camp in South Vietnam. This study was done not only to gain an understanding into their habits and behavior, but out of the necessity to figure out why the native population was unable to deal with them effectively. Rats carry diseases, and often many of the populations living in isolated villages as well as towns die or suffer from the proximity of these animals.

22 G.W.F. Hegel, *Die Lehre vom Sein* (Hamburg: Felix Meiner Verlag GmbH, 1990), figure 3. The Science of Being.

23 Hegel, *Wissenschaft der Logik.*

NOTES FOR CHAPTER 2

1 Immanuel Kant's famous dictum, *"The only irrefutable hypothesis is the human intuition,"* is the only explanation possible for the Noumenon. Hegel and Schopenhauer support this assertion.

2 Detailed information about the articulation and development process is beyond the scope of this book. Refer to Szabolcs M. de Gyurky, *The Cognitive Dynamics of Computer Science* (Hoboken, NJ: John Wiley & Sons, 2006).

3 Ibid.

4 Detailed information about the articulation and development process is beyond the scope of this book. Refer to ibid.

5 Jet Propulsion Laboratory. *Software Management Standards Package: JPL-STD-D-4008 Level II*, Version 3.0. JPL (Pasadena, CA: California Institute of Technology, December 1988).

6 Arthur Schopenhauer, *Die Welt als Wille und Vorstellung*, Zweiter Band (Book Two) (welcher die Ergänzungen zu den vier Büchern des ersten Bandes enthält) (Munich: Deutscher Taschenbuch Verlag), 158.

7 2,819,185,846 mi in the case of Voyager 2 at Neptune.

8 *JPL-Software Management Standard D-4000*; Version 3.0 (Pasadena, CA: Jet Propulsion Laboratory, California Institute of Technology, December, 1988).

9 de Gyurky, *The Cognitive Dynamics of Computer Science*. See the Four Case Studies.

10 We lost a significant spacecraft, Mars Climate Orbiter, because of a mere triviality—a confusion resulting from the conflated usage of Metric and Imperial measures.

11 Immanuel Kant, *Kritik der praktischen Vernunft* (Riga: Johann Friedrich Hartknoch, 1788; reprint, Erlangen: Harald Fischer Verlag, 1984).

12 Immanuel Kant, *Kritik der reinen Vernunft*, with introduction in Latin by Sir Francis Bacon (Königsberg: August Messer, 1787; reprint, Prussian Academy of Science).

13 Immanuel Kant, *Kritik der Urteilskraft* (1790; reprint, Hamburg: Verlag von Felix Meiner, 1924, and Berlin: Deutscher Forschungsgemeinschaft, Herstellung: Lindemann & Lüdecke).

14 The functional requirements of the systems that make up the constellation are at Level I, and their subsystem functional requirements are at Level II.

15 de Gyurky, *The Cognitive Dynamics of Computer Science*. See the TOPEX case study, §14.3.

16 It was a great relief and confirmation that Hegel was completely correct in saying that integral and differential calculus were the keys to modeling human functions mathematically.

17 That is, if the war game, be it a Command Post Exercise (CPX) or Field Training Exercise (FTX), is run honestly and with discipline, which is often not the case.

NOTES FOR CHAPTER 3

1 *JPL-Software Management Standard D-4000*; Version 3.0 (Pasadena, CA: Jet Propulsion Laboratory, California Institute of Technology, December 1988).

2 Peter Sloterdijk, *Philosophie Jezt! Fichte*, Johann Gottlieb (Munich: Eugen Diederichs Verlag, 1996).

3 Arthur Schopenhauer, *Die Welt als Wille und Vorstellung*, Gesamtausgabe [The World as Will and Presentation] (Munich: Deutsche Taschenbuch Verlag GmbH & Co. KG, April 1998), 25. Vorrede zur Zweite Auflage [Prologue to the Second Edition]. §On Absolute Truth and Objective Reality, which is not only a functional process, but the theme, and the logical construction of the Idea and its Substance.

4 Ibid., 15–16. In reference to the driving force of the-search-for-Truth as the *primum mobile* (the principle driving force and motivator) of mental and physical development and progress.

5 Arthur Schopenhauer, *Die Welt als Wille und Vorstellung* (The World as Will and Presentation), Zweiter Band (Volume Two) (Munich: Deutscher Taschenbuch Verlag GmbH, 1988).

6 Ibid., 325.

7 "Spinoza [Letter #58, p.909] says that if a stone which has been projected through the air had consciousness, it would believe that it was moving of its own Will. I add to this only that the stone would be right. The impulse given it is for the stone what the motive is for me, and what in the case of the stone appears as cohesion, gravitation, rigidity, is in its inner nature the same as that which I recognize in myself as Will, and what the stone also, if knowledge were given to it, would recognize as Will."—Arthur Schopenhauer, *The World as Will and Idea*, trans. Haldane and Kemp (Boston: Ticknor ad Co., 1887), 1:164.

8 Schopenhauer, *Die Welt als Wille und Vorstellung* (1998), 288.

9 Ibid., 312.

10 *The American Heritage Dictionary of the English Language*, 4th ed. (Boston: Houghton Mifflin Company, copyright ©2000, updated in 2009, all rights reserved).

11 Note that this is not the Wagnerian story and opera, *Götterdämmerung*, "Twilight of the Gods."

12 Theodore von Kármán, *The Wind and Beyond* (Boston: Little, Brown, 1967), 65, 211–215.

13 Immanuel Kant, *Kritik der reinen Vernunft*, Herausgegeben und Eingeleitet von August Messer (Berlin und Leipzig: Verlag von Th. Knaur Nachf., 1912), 215, 652.

14 Szabolcs M. de Gyurky, *The Cognitive Dynamics of Computer Science* (Hoboken NJ: John Wiley & Sons, 2006), 138 (Acceptable Reality).

15 Schopenhauer, *Die Welt als Wille und Vorstellung* (1998), 428–430.

16 Kant, *Kritik der reinen Vernunft*.

17 Schopenhauer, *Die Welt als Wille und Vorstellung* (1998), 288.

18 The Voyager I spacecraft will pass within 1.6 light years of the star Gliese 445 in approximately 40,000 earth years.

19 G.W.F. Hegel, *Wissenschaft der Logik/Die Lehre vom Sein* (1832) (The Monadic Operating System: Grades and Types of Monads) (Hamburg: Felix Meiner Verlag, 1990), 232–235.

20 Immanuel Kant, *Kritik der reinen Vernunft* (Riga: Hartknoch, 1787–88), 275.

NOTES FOR CHAPTER 4

1 Arthur Schopenhauer, *Die Welt als Wille und Vorstellung*, Zweiter Band, vol. 1 (Munich: Deutsche Taschenbuch Verlag, April 1988), 75.

2 Ibid., 2:204.

3 Immanuel Kant, *Kritik der reinen Vernunft* (Berlin und Leipzig: Th. Knaur Nachf. Verlag, 1912).

4 Immanuel Kant, *Kritik der praktischen Vernunft* (Riga: Johann Friedrich Hartknoch Verlag, 1788).

5 Ibid.

6 It is recognized that there is no way that we can create absolute reality at this point. Absolute reality is achievable only in logic and mathematics.

7 Arthur Schopenhauer, *Die Welt als Wille und Vorstellung*, Zweiter Band (vol. 2) (Munich: Deutsche Taschenbuch Verlag GmbH & Co. KG, 1988), 325, paraphrased.

8 Note: Empirical, based on experience. The philosophical direction where all recognition is traced back to physical experience.

9 Kant, *Kritik der reinen Vernunft*, 82.

10 Floyd Seyward Lear, *Treason in Roman and Germanic Law* (Austin: University of Texas Press, 1965).

11 Theodore Mommsen, *Römisches Strafrecht*. 2 (Leipzig, 1899; reprint, Aalen: Scientia Verlag). *Staats Recht*, Zweiter Unveränderlicher Nachdruck Der Dritte Auflage (second reprint of the third edition) (Austria: Akademische Druck- u. Verlagsanstalt Graz, 1969).

NOTES FOR CHAPTER 5

1 Arthur Schopenhauer, *Die Welt als Wille und Vorstellung* (Zweites Buch) (Munich: Deutscher Taschenbuchverlag, 1998), 315.

2 Arthur Schopenhauer, *Die Welt als Wille und Vorstellung*, vol. 1, Vorrede (Introduction) (München: Deutsche Taschenbuch Verlag GmbH & Co. KG, 1988), 23.

3 G.W.F. Hegel, *Logik: Die Lehre vom Sein* (1832), *Wissenschaft der Logik* (Hamburg: Felix Meiner Verlag, 1985), 150

4 Theodore von Kármán and Lee Edson, *The Wind and Beyond* (Boston: Little, Brown, 1967), 211.

5 See Flourens' experiments on live animals. Refer to chap. 3, The Architecture of The Will system, §3.7.1 The Survival Subsystem.

6 G.W.F. Hegel, *Wissenschaft der Logik (Erster Teil Die objektive Logik), Die Lehre vom Sein* (1832) (Hamburg: Felix Meiner Verlag, 1990), 57.

7 Tracy Kidder, *The Soul of a New Machine*, 2nd ed. (Modern Library, 1997).

8 Schopenhauer, *Die Welt als Wille und Vorstellung*, vol. 2 (1988), 315.

9 Ibid.

10 Even self-modifying hardware systems, in their essence, are hardwired.

11 Schopenhauer, *Die Welt als Wille und Vorstellung*. Zweiter Band (1998), 340.

12 Examples of optimal languages for the mind of the constellation to communicate among its various systems would be on the order of Latin, or perhaps Greek or Hungarian, since they are very rich in structure, with subject and predicate, and integrated into object recognition. Strict English, too, could be pressed into service. Only such advanced languages can support speculative and formal logic, as Hegel points out.

NOTES FOR CHAPTER 6

1 Arthur Schopenhauer, *Die Welt als Wille und Vorstellung*, Erster Band (Munich: Deutscher Taschenbuch Verlag GmbH & KG, 1988), 43.
2 G.W.F. Hegel, *Wissenschaft der Logik, Die Lehre vom Sein* (Hamburg: Felix Meiner Verlag, 1990), 128, 129.
3 What does this great Hegelian assertion, "negation of the negation," mean to computer science? It means that the boundaries of all ideas are eliminated, and one may drive ideas and concepts beyond the rules that have been established.
4 Hegel, *Wissenschaft der Logik*, XVIII. This is the dissertation on the power and structure of the languages in which we think.
5 Szabolcs M. de Gyurky, *The Cognitive Dynamics of Computer Science* (Hoboken, NJ: John Wiley & Sons, 2006), "Achieving Sufficient Reality," 49.

NOTES FOR CHAPTER 7

1 Arthur Schopenhauer, *Die Welt als Wille und Vorstellung*, Zweiter Band, Zweiter Hälfte Die Lehre von der Abstrakten Vorstellung Oder Dem Denkens (Munich: Deutscher Taschenbuch Verlag, 1988), 88. "Books cannot replace experience!"
2 Manfred Geier, *Kants Welt* (Reinbek bei Hamburg: Rowohlt Taschenbuch Verlag, 2005), 166.
3 Szabolcs M. de Gyurky, *The Cognitive Dynamics of Computer Science* (Hoboken, NJ: John Wiley & Sons, 2006).
4 Aristotle, *The Works of Aristotle,* vol. 1: *Categoriae and De interpretatione*, ed. E. M. Edghill (London: Oxford Clarendon Press, Amen House, E.G.4, 1928).
5 Ibid.

NOTES FOR CHAPTER 8

1 Raymund Schmidt, *Kant: Die drei Kritiken* (Stuttgart: Alfred Kröner Verlag, 1975), 78.
2 G.W. F. Hegel, *Wissenschaft der Logik. Die Lehre vom Sein* (1832) (Hamburg: Felix Meiner Verlag, 1990), 156.
3 Arthur Schopenhauer, *Die Welt als Wille und Vorstellung*, 320.
4 Because the autonomous system will be human-like (and advanced, if designed properly) in its thought performance, abilities, and psychological needs, it indeed *cannot be alone*. It must have a group of like companions to navigate, fly the spacecraft, do repairs, build parts, and simply to prevent depression and isolation, which are part and parcel of space travel. Thus, we arrive at the need to examine the parameters of regulating coexistence in a relatively confined space over incomprehensibly long periods of time.

5 Hegel, *Wissenschaft der Logik. Die Lehre vom Sein*, Erster Band (vol. 1), 17–30.

6 This is a very important software design concept from Aristotle's time, and then through the great thinkers of classical philosophy. Thought fragments are a lot like pieces of a jigsaw puzzle coming from the external and internal sensors in an unending stream into the mind. They are filtered by some of the systems, such as the Intellect, Reason, and Will—if they are in operation—and projected onto the Presentation for viewing, cataloging, and compiling, and are then stored for further enhancement by categories. This process is a miracle of the human mind and can be replicated in software design as well. The Idea is the task, and the Concept is the design.

NOTES FOR CHAPTER 9

1 Szabolcs M. de Gyurky, *The Cognitive Dynamics of Computer Science* (Hoboken, NJ: John Wiley & Sons, 2006), 25.

2 Hjalmar Schacht, *1933 Wie eine Demokratie stirbt* [How a Democracy Dies] (Düsseldorf: Econ-Verlag, 1968).

3 Hjalmar Schacht, *Guttentagsche Sammlung Nr. 26 Münz- und Bankgesetzgebung* [German Coinage and Banking Laws] (Deutscher Reichsgesetze Nr. 26, Berlin; Leipzig: Walter de Gruyter, 1926).

4 The Leadership Reaction Course of the 7th U.S. Army Non-Commissioned Officers Academy at the Flint Kaserne in Bad Tölz, Germany.

5 NCOs from the rank of Sergeant E-5 through the rank of Master Sergeant E-8. In some cases, junior enlisted men were selected if they were about to attend Officer Candidate School or were about to be promoted to Corporal E-4.

6 Immanuel Kant, *Kritik der Urteilskraft* (Hamburg: Verlag von Felix Meiner, 1954).

7 Arthur Schopenhauer, *Die Welt als Wille und Vorstellung*, Erster Band, Drittes Buch (Munich: Deutscher Taschenbuchverlag GmbH, 1998), 324.

8 Ibid., 327.

9 Schopenhauer, *Die Welt als Wille und Vorstellung*, Erstes Buch, 43.

10 Whether one likes Napoleon Bonaparte as a person or not, it must be admitted that the Battle of Waterloo itself was well planned. By the time of Waterloo, Napoleon's incomparable chief of staff, Marshall Louis Berthier, had committed suicide by jumping off the balcony of his hotel in Paris. His new chief of staff did not understand command and control, and the execution of the battle plan was a disaster. A well-trained, superbly qualified, and experienced staff is as important to a successful outcome of a war, battle, or project as an equally experienced and qualified project manager or commander-in-chief. When one sees cost overruns, botched wars or projects, one must blame the project manager or commanding general—no excuses! Amateurism is not a signal for success.

11 de Gyurky *The Cognitive Dynamics of Computer Science*, 41.

12 Schopenhauer, *Die Welt als Wille und Vorstellung*, Zweiter Band (vol. 2), Zweites Buch (book 2), Kapitel 22 (chap. 22), 325, on the objective analysis of the Will.

13 Johan Gottlieb Fichte, *Fichte, Ausgewählte und vorgestellt von Günter Schulte* (Munich: Dietrichs, 1996), 143.

14 Immanuel Kant, *Die drei Kritiken*, Eine kommentierte Auswahl von Raymund Schmidt (Stuttgart: Alfred Kröner Verlag, 1975), 262.

15 Immanuel Kant, *Kritik der Urteilskraft*, Herausgegeben von Karl Vorländer (Hamburg: Verlag von Felix Meiner, 1954), 35, 256.

16 Ibid., 246.

17 There is also the option of designing two separate decision processors. However, for practical purposes, we describe one decision processor with the product or result being either an *a priori* or *a posteriori* decision.

18 G.W.F. Hegel, *Wissenschaft der Logik. Die Lehre vom Sein* (1832) (Hamburg: Felix Meiner Verlag, 1990), 82.

19 Raymund Schmidt, *Kant: Die Drei Kritiken* (The Three Critiques), Eine kommentierte Auswahl (Stuttgart: Alfred Kröner Verlag, 1975), 100–110.

20 "Some arms taken at Bath in the year 1715, distinguished from all others in the Tower, by having what is called dog locks; that is, a kind of lock with a catch to prevent their going off at half-cock."—*London and Its Environs Described* (London: R. and J. Dodsley, 1761).

21 Kant, *Kritik der Urteilskraft*, 33.

22 Schopenhauer, *Die Welt als Wille und Vorstellung*, Erster Band, Anhang, 598.

23 Ibid., 606.

24 German Wehrmacht (Armed Forces) Technical Manual, *Handbuch für Kraftfahrer*, Bearbeitet nach dem neuesten Stande des Kraftfahrzeug und Motorenbauens (Berlin: E.S. Mittler Sohn, 1939), 152.

25 Kant, *Kritik der Urteilskraft*, 48.

26 Ibid., 125.

27 Schopenhauer, *Die Welt als Wille und Vorstellung*, Zweiter Band, Zweites Buch, Kapitel 19, p. 280.

28 Kant, *Kritik der Urteilskraft*, 101.

NOTES FOR CHAPTER 10

1 G.W.F. Hegel, *Wissenschaft der Logik. Die Lehre vom Sein* (1832), Erster Teil. Die objektive Logik (Hamburg: Felix Meiner Verlag, 1985), 26.

2 Such as "emergent behavior."

3 Arthur Schopenhauer, *Die Welt als Wille und Vorstellung*, Erstes Buch, Erste Betrachtung (Munich: Deutscher Taschenbuch Verlag GmbH & Co. KG, April 1998), 75.

4 Note: In organic and primitive systems, the Will begins the accumulation of rules, laws, and axioms simply by an auto-reflex as a negative rule, for example, of not touching a fire a second time. Understanding that moisture for a plant is good, it directs its roots like an Acacia tree to the nearest source of water, deep in the soil.

5 Immanuel Kant, *Kritik der reinen Vernunft* (Berlin: Verlag von Th. Knaur Nachf., circa 1912), 243–248.

6 G.W.F. Hegel, *Wissenschaft der Logik. Die Lehre vom Sein* 1832 (Hamburg: Felix Meiner Verlag, 1990), 57.

7 Baltasar Gracian, *The Wisdom of Baltasar Gracian: A Practical Manual for Good and Perilous Times*, adapted and edited by J. Leonard Kaye (New York: Pocket Books, 1992), 67.

8 Charlton T. Lewis and Charles Short, *A Latin Dictionary*, founded on Andrews' edition of Freund's *Latin Dictionary* (Oxford: Clarendon Press, 1879).

9 Ibid.

10 Hegel, *Wissenschaft der Logik* (1990)

11 Ibid., 27.

12 Ibid., 27.

13 Schopenhauer, *Die Welt als Wille und Vorstellung*, 84–85.

14 Immanuel Kant, *Kritik der reinen Vernunft, Herausgegeben* (Published) von August Messer, Professor der Philosophie an der Universität Gießen (Berlin: Verlag von Th. Knaur Nachf., circa 1922), 275–276.

15 Hegel, *Wissenschaft der Logik* (1990), 227.

16 Ibid., 43.

17 Ibid., 39.

18 Ibid., 583.

19 Consider an autonomous system capable of exploring deep space, one entrusted with the construction of Mission Support Sites (MSS) on planets or asteroids. An MSS capable of supporting human life is as advanced an undertaking as we can contemplate. When the construction is accomplished by autonomous systems, the communication issue looms even more important than were the task done by human beings. This communication cannot be a slipshod affair as we humans use among ourselves. We cannot risk the lives of our spacecraft crews due to misunderstandings. On unmanned missions such as the Voyagers, which stretch into an indefinite number of years, we cannot subject them to accidental destruction because of our carelessness.

20 Hegel, *Wissenschaft der Logik* (1990), 230, 235, 314.

21 *Malchi Vita Pythagorae*, ed. Ritterhus (Amsterdam: Moderatus aus Cadix, circa 1560).

22 Hegel, W. *Wissenschaft der Logik* (1990), 225–227.

23 The reason the Will system is addressed here in a monologue mode is because it is the *prius*. All living things have a Will. In the animal world, a Nexus Cogitationis does not exist, so the Will develops the Reason, which is, in the primitive sense, the dos and don'ts. In humans, it can be developed into axioms, laws, rules, and so on. We are using architectural license and the discretion of systems engineering in this instance.

24 Jet Propulsion Laboratory, *Software Management Standards Package Level II JPL D-4006*, Version 3.0 (Pasadena, CA: Jet Propulsion Laboratory, California Institute of Technology, December 1988).

25 Ibid.

26 Hegel, *Wissenschaft der Logik, Erster Band: Die Lehre vom Sein* (1990), 585.

NOTES FOR EPILOGUE

1 Arthur Schopenhauer, *Die Welt als Wille und Vorstellung*, Gesamtausgabe, Erster Band (Munich: Deutsche Taschenbuch Verlag GmbH & Co. KG, 1998), 552.

2 G.W.F. Hegel, *Wissenschaft der Logik, Die Lehre vom Sein*, Erster Teil: The Objective Logic (Hamburg: Felix Meiner Verlag, 1990), 46.

3 Immanuel Kant, *Kritik der reinen Vernunft*, Herausgegeben und eingeleitet von August Messer, Professor der Philosophie und der Universität Gießen (Berlin und Leipzig: Verlag von Th. Knaur Nachf, 1925), 287.

4 Hegel, *Wissenschaft der Logik. Die Lehre vom Sein* (1832), 48. It would be negligent not to quote Hegel's opinion on Kant's philosophy: "Die Kantische Philosophie dient so als ein Polster für die Trägheit des Denkens, die sich damit beruhigt, daß bereits alles bewiesen und abgetan sei."—"The philosophy of Kant serves as the protective upholstery against the sluggish thinkers who find comfort and relaxation in the conviction that everything has been proven and settled."

5 Schopenhauer, *Die Welt als Wille und Vorstellung*, 325.

6 Ibid., 340.

7 Ibid., 341.

8 Szabolcs M. de Gyurky, *The Cognitive Dynamics of Computer Science/Cost-Effective Large Scale Software Development* (Hoboken, NJ: John Wiley & Sons, 2006), 55–78

9 Hegel, *Wissenschaft der Logik, Die Lehre vom Sein* (1832), die Erster Teil: Die Objektive Logik, Erster Band/Die Lehre vom Sein, 22.

Index

The Autonomous System: A Foundational Synthesis of the Sciences of the Mind, First Edition. Szabolcs Michael de Gyurky and Mark A. Tarbell.